The Magic World of the Xhosa

The Magic World of the Xhosa

Aubrey Elliott

CHARLES SCRIBNER'S SONS

NEW YORK

Contents

To Margaret and Wayne

Acknowledgements

In expressing my appreciation to the people who made this book possible, I would, in particular, like to thank them not only for the valuable time they afforded me, but for the spirit in which they gave that time. In a work of this nature many different people in different walks of life each contribute a share of some kind, and a feature of these various contributions which inspired me throughout the years which it took to complete the work, was everyone's genuine interest in it. This interest, I felt, was a common desire on their part to help preserve for our country and for the future, something of the colourful way of life of the people about whom it is written.

In expressing this gratitude, I think it is fitting, first, to mention the owners of the farms on which much of the research for *The Magic World of the Xhosa* was done and where most of the photographs were taken. Their help laid the foundations of the book and I cannot emphasise too strongly the value of their co-operation. In alphabetical order, they are:

Mr B. Bursey, my brother Hilton, Mr R. King, Mr M. Mills, Mr R. E. D. Mountfort and Mr B. Robinson.

Then I would like to thank the following for their kind help, each in their own field. Their names are also in alphabetical order:

Mr E. H. Bigalke of the East London museum who was able to furnish me with much useful information.

Mrs Lesley Elliott, who played an important part in getting me launched on this book.

My young son, Wayne, who accompanied me for many thousands of miles to, and in, 'Xhosa country'. His boyish questions about the customs and habits of the Xhosa often set me thinking in new and interesting directions and resulted in features of this book which might otherwise not have been there. His help too, on the photographic side, was invaluable because often, when time was not on my side, he gave me assistance without which I could not have handled my three cameras. In fact, he often took over one of the cameras and used it for me.

Mr F. J. Malan, who edited the spelling of the Xhosa words I have used. Furthermore, he read the manuscript in detail and, as a result of several of his suggestions I was able to bring in finer points of interest which were of definite benefit to the book.

Mr J. S. Malan for his constructive criticism of the last four chapters, which deal with the magic and religion of the tribe.

Mr Lolombela Mbangeli, a Xhosa man who is wrapped up in the rites and customs of his people. He is a traditionalist in the true sense and rules his family in orthodox Xhosa style. He follows the old rites, believes in Xhosa ideas and makes sacrifices to his ancestors. He was a wealth of information to me, for he carries, in his head, almost as if in indexed form, a detailed knowledge of all the traditional practices and ideas of his people.

Mr A. Meintjies of Macleantown. Mr Meintjies spent a lifetime in the heart of the area where much of the Xhosa tribal life, still in the purest form, is to be found. He speaks their language as well as the Xhosa themselves and he tells many interesting stories of episodes which he has experienced, and which arose out of Xhosa beliefs, behaviour and customs. He knows the procedures of their ceremonies, the ways of their witch-doctors and what is likely to emerge when a Xhosa's superstition runs riot. I drew much in this book from his vast store of knowledge of the Xhosa.

Mrs Madeline Murgatroyd who saw a collection of my Xhosa photographs when the idea of this book was still taking shape in my mind. Her insistence that the book was needed, her confidence that it would be accepted and her continued persistence thereafter that I should write it, all had their effect and helped me finally to build my own deep interests.

Mr D. C. Odendaal, of Pretoria, whose interest in the work and help in the final stages of its preparation proved of particular value.

Dr. Barbara Tyrrell for her sustained interest in the book through much of its period of preparation, particularly at the time when she was tremendously busy herself in completing her great work of art, *The Tribal Peoples of Southern Africa*. She was always generous enough to discuss my progress and problems with me.

Dr. N. J. van Warmelo who, with his intense knowledge of the bantu peoples of the Republic, often put me on the right track when I might easily otherwise have confused some point of fact.

Mr M. Vosloo, of Pretoria, who spent untold hours reading and re-reading my work as it progressed, checking for technical errors and suggesting occasional amendments, and all the while showing a profound interest which never failed to spur me on.

Professor Monica Wilson, who gave up much of her time to reading my manuscript and for making corrections and suggestions. Her specialised help was much appreciated.

On the photographic side I wish to thank the following:

Mr C. A. van Tilburg who, with infinite care, processed nearly one thousand colour pictures which I took of the Xhosa in the course of the compilation of the book.

Mr E. Harper who, with fine knowledge of the intricacies of photography, expertly copied numerous pictures for my working purposes and for my records.

The Pretoria Photographic Society for the grounding they gave me in the principles of photography. Their early guidance in this field contributed in no small measure towards my ultimately obtaining the coveted award of an Associateship of the Photographic Society of Southern Africa (A.P.S. (S.A.).)

I feel I would be lacking in appreciation if I were to omit to mention the numerous Xhosa tribesmen—men, women and children—who, with endless patience and goodwill, not only allowed me to photograph them, but gave me their sincere co-operation. This also goes for those of them whom I questioned in the course of my research. Their help was of inestimable value.

In the same way I would like to thank those of my friends whose continued interest in this work kept me at it when otherwise I might easily have relaxed my efforts.

For typing my manuscript, my gratitude goes to Miss Rosie Funga. She deciphered my handwriting, typed and re-typed and filled in my corrections and amendments. The book never seemed to tire her and what was particularly important, she convinced me that she was enjoying it.

My final expression of appreciation is to Mrs Irma von Geusau who typed the index and also the captions of the pictures shown. In addition, she assisted me in the recording and classifying of the numerous photographs out of which those for the book were ultimately chosen.

Foreword

The Author has described himself as a Ciskei farmer's son who grew up among the Xhosa people.

This simple pen picture is one which might apply to a vast number of South Africans who grow up in close proximity to rural African peoples. Most of us work side by side with Africans. We have a smattering of their languages, marvel a little at their strange beliefs and customs – and leave it at that.

Aubrey Elliott is a farmer's son with a difference. In his day-by-day boyhood among the Xhosa he learned their language well and, with a rare perceptiveness, must have sensed at an early age the strange wonderland of the minds of the people who dwelt in kraals on his father's farm. He observed and he strove to understand. He has since recorded with the camera and with the pen.

This book, today, is the rich harvest of the years. The Xhosa of the Red Blanket come alive in the sympathetic magic of his pen and their beauty is preserved for all time in the artistry of his photographs.

Little has been written on the Xhosa, other than of purely scientific nature. This book, of profoundly scientific interest, having the authenticity of the eye witness, reads with the ease of a fairy tale in real life. Here, preserved for the future, is material for science, art and ballet. Aubrey Elliott reveals a mysterious world of ancestral spirits, sprites and demons and of the web of custom which encompasses the daily life of these Xhosa who have entrusted to him the telling of their story. This book, with its beauty and insight, proves the author worthy of their trust and offers to its readers a deeper understanding, not only of the Xhosa people, but of all tribal bantu, whose beliefs and customs have a basic similarity.

In the course of my studies of tribal life my path has many times crossed that of the author. In his keen search for knowledge and understanding he exhibits the rare quality of being able to 'put himself into the other man's shoes'. With this talent, his camera and his deep knowledge of the Xhosa language he has produced a book which I have great pleasure in recommending to all who seek to understand the strange riddles of Africa.

BARBARA TYRRELL

Introduction

The Xhosa people constitute one of the Republic of South Africa's biggest and best known bantu tribes. Their language has remained pure through the centuries and it is lending its influence in ever-increasing measures to other bantu peoples throughout the country. Today, in keeping with the pace of development in the country, the Xhosa are moving fast into modern civilisation. They are filling schools and churches; many are buying motor cars and, in increasing numbers, they are moving away from their old tribal homes into the cities. But there is still a hard core of the colourful old pagan tribesmen, who are known as the 'Red Blankets', to be found in the more remote corners of the area in which the Xhosa people traditionally live. They are the last of their kind and they depict the end of an era in Xhosa history. Not many years from now the interesting old 'raw' Xhosa of the Red Blanket tradition will have disappeared completely, taking with him his picturesque way of life and leaving only as a memory the centuries-old tribal rites of his people.

It is about the Red Blankets that this book is written and the idea in it is to capture, in photographs and in print, something of their fascinating ways of life before the opportunity is lost forever. It tells of their elaborate tribal rites, their witchdoctors and sorcerers, of their belief in magic and medicines and of their worship of the spirits of their ancestors.

In presenting these facts, I have attempted not to burden the reader with an excess of technical detail and I lay no claim to have covered every intricate aspect of the Xhosa tribe's highly complex system of beliefs and customs. I have used Xhosa words sparingly in my text in order not to labour the reading, but those which I have included were put in for the specific purpose of retaining the original sense and importance of the word, particularly to the more serious reader or student of Xhosa. There is a glossary of Xhosa words.

The Xhosa were the first bantu people (as opposed to Hottentots and Bushmen) to be encountered by the early white pioneers in their move up the coast of the Cape Colony and they are the people against whom many fierce Kaffir wars were fought in the early settler days in South Africa. The Xhosa tribe is a united one which is made up of many clans who combine into a proud race of people. In their known history they have never been defeated by or made subservient to any other bantu tribe and, unlike so many of South Africa's black peoples, they were never at any stage broken by the powerful Zulu Chief Shaka.

The customs, beliefs and rites in the Xhosa tribe are basically the same throughout the tribe, but there are minor variations in ritual procedure within the different clans and, sometimes, even in family units. The information in this book is based on research done in the Ciskei section of the tribe. The Ciskei is broadly the area in which the Xhosa live South of the Great Kei River down the coastal strip past the port of East London. It is where I grew up as a farmer's son and where I learned the ways of the Xhosa from childhood and their language at the same time as I learned my own.

SCENE IN KAFFIRLAND, MAY 1.

Chapter 1   In Past Years

Left: A Kaffir settlement

The origin of the sketch of Sandile is unknown. Sandile (1820–29 May 1878) was a Rarabe chief who played an important part in several of the Frontier wars.

The bantu population, that is the black people, of the Republic of South Africa is made up of numerous different tribes spread out over various parts of the country. Each speaks its own language, or a derivation of a common basic language, and many of the tribes differ from each other quite noticeably in their physical characteristics. Men of any particular tribe are always proud of their respective nationalities and rate loyalty to their chiefs and to their clans among the first essentials in their code of honour.

The various tribes live in quite separate localities and in usually well-defined areas; for instance the Zulu people live in Zululand and Natal; a tribe called the Ndebele over a wide area of the Eastern Transvaal; the Pondo have their home in the rugged, inaccessible hills on the East coast of the Transkei; the Bomvana live lower down in the same territory and the Xhosa in the South-Eastern part of the Cape Colony, which includes two districts of the Transkei.

The Xhosa are one of the biggest and best known of all the bantu tribes in the Republic and they have the longest association with the white race in the country as they were the first bantu people, as opposed to Hottentots and Bushmen, to come into contact with the early European settlers in the Cape.

The 'Red Blankets'

Today, the Xhosa tribe lives on the Republic's South-Eastern seaboard in an area stretching for approximately two hundred miles along the coast, from about the Keiskama River to the Bashee River—with the port of East London in the middle—and varying in depth, inland, up to about a hundred miles. Thirty miles up the coast from East London, the Great Kei River cuts through Xhosa territory to divide it into two parts: the Ciskei on the South bank and the Transkei on the North.

Because of their colourful dress, which is basically a cotton or woollen blanket dyed a deep-brick colour with red ochre, these people are known as 'Red Blankets'. I have not been able to establish how and when their custom of ochre-dyeing their clothes started, but it is interesting to note that back in 1822 in the Albany district of the Cape Colony, they were bartering ivory for red ochre powder for this purpose.

The tribe is a large, colourful and proud one who never, in their recorded history, have been conquered by or made subservient to any other bantu tribe. Today, they still practise customs and rites which are centuries old and they live by a code which has been passed down through the generations from father to son. The Xhosa are steeped in superstition and witchcraft, and magic rules their lives.

Their National Suicide—*Nongqause*

The power which magic and mystery holds over them is perhaps never better illustrated than in the incident of their 'national suicide' or—as it is called in their own language— '*Nongqause*'. It is so important an event in the life of these people that I find it impossible to leave out of this book even though, otherwise, I have made no reference to the early history of the Xhosa. Apart from the fact that the episode of *Nongqause* so well illustrates the Xhosa tribesman's unshakeable belief in magic, it also had a bearing on the geographical distribution of the tribe as it ended after this 'suicide', which took place in the years 1856 and 1857.

In 1856 the Xhosa were spoiling for another war with the white settlers on the Cape's frontiers and, to add fuel to their simmering restlessness, their cattle started dying of lungsickness, for which they blamed the witchcraft of the English who were at this time governing the Cape Colony.

The event, which subsequently became known as *Nongqause*, was one which many believe was engineered by leaders among the Xhosa to stir up their population into the right frame of mind for an all-out war to drive the English into the sea. But whether this was, in fact, the case or whether *Nongqause* was the outcome of Xhosa credulity and a deep belief in the supernatural, will never now be known.

One day in May 1856 a young girl of about fourteen whose name was Nongqause (the Xhosa version is Unongqawuza) came back from the river where she had been to fetch water and said that, while there, she had seen some men who were quite different from ordinary men. Nongqause was a daughter of a counsellor to Chief Kreli (Sarili) and her father's brother was a man named Umhlakaza*, who claimed to be a prophet. Umhlakaza decided to go down to the river to see these people for himself. He found them there and they told him he should go back home and purify himself with medicines, sacrifice an ox to the spirits and return again to them on the fourth day.

When he went back after being purified, he found the men there again and amongst them was his brother who had been dead for many years. They told him they had come from far-off battlefields across the sea and that they were invincible. They claimed to be the sworn enemies of the white man and said that they would help the Xhosa to overcome them if

---

* I have also seen it reported that Nongqause was the *daughter* of Umhlakaza

they would obey the spirits and do everything they were told. Umhlakaza, they said, would be the medium between them, the spirits, and the Xhosa rulers.

A fine description of the opening chapters of this drama is given in the book *Reminiscences of Kaffir Life and History* by Charles Brownlee, published in 1896. Charles Brownlee was Gaika Commissioner at the time and accordingly witnessed the tragedy. The Gaikas are an important Xhosa clan whose leader was Chief Sandile. The report reads: Nongqause 'professed to have held converse with the spirits of the old Kaffir heroes—who had witnessed with sorrow the ruin of their race from the oppression of their conquerors; and as they would no longer be silent spectators of the wrongs and insults, it was their intention to come to the rescue and save their progeny from destruction. They would appear and move in the flesh among their people, but they would not do so unless the Kaffir nation would exterminate all cattle both great and small, with the exception of horses and dogs. All grain was to be thrown away, neither was there to be cultivation. The advent of the resurrection would be pre-

ceded by the frightful whirlwind which would sweep off all Kaffirs who refused to obey the orders of the spirits. At first the Kaffir nation was stunned. The sacrifice seemed too great. Tidings of the marvellous sights witnessed near Umhlakaza's village filled the country. The horns of oxen were said to be seen peeping from beneath the rushes which grew around a swampy pool near the village of the seer; and from a subterranean cave were heard the bellowing and knocking of the horns of cattle impatient to rise. Kreli declared he had seen a celebrated horse of Umhlakaza's long since dead but now alive. A child of the prophet had also come back from the dead. There were those who said they had actually seen the risen heroes emerge from the Indian Ocean, some on foot, some on horseback, passing in silent parade before them, then sinking again among the tossings of the restless waves. Sometimes they were seen rushing through the air in the wild chase as of old. Then again they were seen marshalled in battle array. The horrors to befall the unbelievers were enlarged upon. White men would be turned into frogs, mice and ants.

15

One can imagine the effect of this upon an intensely superstitious people.'

Elsewhere in the book it says: 'Armies were seen reviewing on the sea, others were sailing in umbrellas . . .'

The first message that Umhlakaza gave was that no one was to have anything more to do with witchcraft and that families were to start killing their fattest cattle and begin feasting.

Chief Kreli sent messages far and wide among the Xhosa that they should kill and eat. The crowds began to work themselves into a frenzy of excitement. Many other chiefs obeyed but some would have nothing to do with the orders, and the advocates of slaughter said of these that they would die with the whites when the chosen time of annihilation came.

When Nongqause went back to the stream, she said she could hear strange rumblings under her feet and her uncle Umhlakaza said these were the voices of the spirits discussing the affairs of the people of the earth.

For months the slaughter went on resulting in starvation in many areas. Yet the people still believed and continued to kill.

Other minor prophets sprang up and one of these was a girl of nine, called Nonkosi, who was partly Hottentot and she claimed that she could hear the spirits talking when she stood in the side waters of the Umpongo River near the present village of Macleantown. Later, after her parents had died of starvation, she confessed to the English that men close to the local chief had been responsible for her making the statements, which were not true.

Then a man, Maqoma, who was Chief Sandile's brother, professed that he had seen and spoken to two old counsellors who were long since dead and they commanded Sandile, who had so far resisted slaughtering, to kill his cattle or perish with the white enemy.

By this time Umhlakaza (the uncle of Nongqause) had given the order that every living animal except horses, which could be used for war, must be killed and all crops and grain destroyed. Great glory and riches, he said, would come to

A skirmish with Kaffirs.

Far left: A young Xhosa wearing a splendid headdress.

Left: The clay paint on this Xhosa's face has no particular significance—it is purely decorative, although the woman says "it does keep her cool".

Below: A girl of the Gqunukwebe clan near East London. Her body is decorated with red ochre but the light colour of her face is evidence of the Hottentot influence which is particularly strong in her clan.

those who obeyed. But, he added, the punishment of those who did not obey would be that the sky would fall on them or an enormous wind would arise and blow them into the sea. This was the same fate as would befall the white people.

It has been suggested that 200,000 head of cattle were killed by the fanatic Xhosa at this time. While their blind superstitious beliefs motivated perhaps most of the killings, it seems that much of the action was organised to stir the tribesmen into a frenzy before they threw themselves on the white population.

By the end of 1856, the tribesmen were already dying in their thousands yet those who still had anything to kill blindly continued to kill, and then sat down, to die of star-

vation. But the rewards they expected were unbounded. New crops would spring out of the ground and great herds of cattle would come thundering across the earth; the cattle would be more fat and beautiful than anything ever seen before and they would be free of disease. At the beginning of 1857, great cattle byres were built by everyone to receive the new herds, new milk sacks were made from skins and huts were strengthened and re-thatched against the hurricane that would blow the disbelievers and the whites into the sea.

Umhlakaza was to nominate the appointed day when the cattle would return and the crops spring forth and the dead return to earth, but he kept on postponing the date

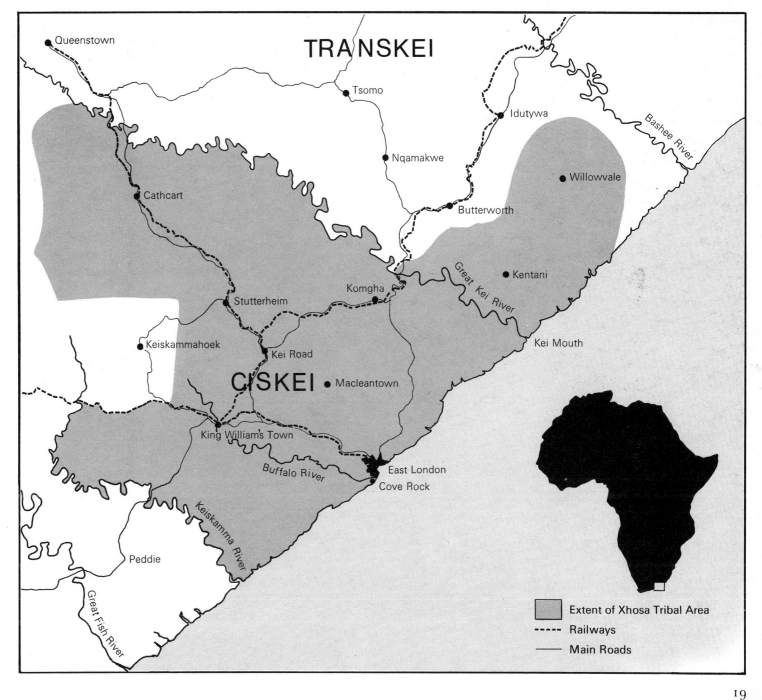

Left: A tranquil scene in the lovely Kei Road area where the rolling hills are clad with masses of flowering mimosa trees at certain times of the year. On their leaves great caterpillars feed and then weave around themselves cocoons which the Xhosa boys collect and make into dancing rattles for their legs.

Right: Map of the Xhosa area.

Queenstown

TRANSKEI

Tsomo

Idutywa

Bashee River

Nqamakwe

Willowvale

Cathcart

Butterworth

Kentani

Great Kei River

Komgha

Stutterheim

Kei Mouth

Keiskammahoek

Kei Road

CISKEI   Macleantown

King William's Town

Buffalo River

East London

Cove Rock

Keiskamma River

Peddie

Great Fish River

Extent of Xhosa Tribal Area

- - - Railways

—— Main Roads

Left: Women gather for a chat over a can of home-made beer. It is customary to pass the one can around in the same way as the pipes go backwards and forwards. The different colours of the blankets denote different clans or, in some cases, the areas of residence. The hut in the background is a storeroom—the residential hut is much bigger.

Right: Cove Rock, the centre of many Xhosa myths. In 1856 the Xhosa slaughtered tens of thousands of their cattle following the visions of a young child prophetess named Nongqause. The local tribesmen at the time believed that great new herds would come thundering out of the sea through this gateway. The Xhosa also say that Cove Rock is the home of the Chiefs of the mysterious "People of the River" and that, in the raging waters on the seaward side of the rock, they guard vast treasures from ships wrecked over the centuries.

Far left: A pipemaker; a witch-doctor's assistant/learner; a witch-doctor and a matmaker.

Left: An elder Xhosa tribesman with his two wives. The wives' respective huts are in the background. In many families it is traditional for the heir to have more than one wife.

while there were still cattle to kill. Then, at last, he chose 18th February 1857 as the day of the resurrection because he considered on that day the moon would be right.

At first, he said that two blood-red suns would come up, but then he changed his mind and decided that there would only be one sun, and that it would move around in the sky and re-set in the east and the hurricanes would then sweep the earth.

The white colonists in the meantime, expecting the worst, made all preparations to defend themselves against a Xhosa attack. At the same time, where possible, the Government built up large stores of food to feed the starving Xhosa people who were going headlong into self-destruction.

On the night before the appointed day, thousands of emaciated Xhosa tribesmen rejoiced, danced and sang throughout the night as they waited for the new day to dawn with its rewards.

Other tribesmen were too afraid of the hurricane that was expected to descend on them to go out and so shut themselves up in their huts. According to the original idea, all the fighting men were supposed to assemble on this night under the pretence of waiting for the resurrection, but, in fact, with the intention of launching their attack from there. This was not done, probably either through lack of adequate organisation or because of their lack of stamina.

The day dawned and the sun rose as usual. Despair descended on the hushed crowds. Hearts sank and the horrible realisation of their fate came home to the thousands. They hoped even then that, perhaps, later in the day Umhlakaza's prediction would come true, but they waited in vain.

Their only hope of salvation now lay with the white colonists whom they had hoped to annihilate, and they flocked to their territory in thousands where they humbly begged food from the farmers.

Families were wrecked and dispersed and fights broke out over the tiniest fragments of food. The lame and old were left to die while everyone who was able fended for him or herself as best they could. Plants and herbs were dug up and eaten and even the hide milk sacks were cooked and eaten. Stories from this period record such incidents as entire families waiting, without hope, for death and other families, more desperate, turning to cannibalism in order to live.

The main instigator of this great tragedy, Umhlakaza, himself died of hunger, but Nongqause survived and lived to see out the horrors she had played the original part in creating. But she would never afterwards, they say, talk of the event and so it was not learned whether she had in fact been an instrument of warmongers, whether she had set out to draw attention to herself or whether she had been overcome by her own imagination. Whatever the reason, her name will be linked for centuries with one of the greatest disasters the tribe could ever have brought on itself.

Movement to the Farms

Apart from the thousands who lost their lives in the Ciskei, the districts of Butterworth, Nqamakwe, Idutywa and Tsomo in the Transkei were depopulated, so that, today, the only true Xhosa districts left in this area, north of the Great Kei River, are those of Kentani and Willowvale.

With their striking power broken, their fighting spirit gone, starving and hungry, those who were able made their way out of traditional Xhosa territory, where they had lived under the sovereignty of their own chiefs, to the white-owned farms of the Ciskei where they were now given food and work. This was a major movement in Xhosa history because it consolidated a large percentage of their people on the farms of the Cape Colony where their descendants, in vastly increased numbers, still live today, over a century later. They form a large part of the Xhosa in the Ciskei among whom the research for this book was done. ..

Hottentot Influence

In the Ciskei today, the Xhosa live and work on white-owned farms and also stay in portions of the territory which, over the years, have remained traditionally Xhosa and where they continue to till the land for themselves in the same way as they do in the Transkei, north of the Great Kei River.

In their own early Cape history, clans of the Xhosa merged

with several Hottentot tribes and so, today, they have a goodly proportion of Hottentot in their veins. The effect of this was to give them a lighter skin tone than many other bantu tribes in the Republic have, and it was also said to have sharpened their intelligence because the Hottentots were regarded as being more intelligent than the bantu.

A particular instance of intermingling of the two races occurred in the case of the Hottentot tribe known as the Damaqua. By the mid-1770's they had ceased to exist as a separate entity after having intermarried over a period with the Tinde clan of the Xhosa.

The present Gqunukwebe clan of the Xhosa, which lives in the Alice area and down towards East London, actually had its origin in a fusion of Xhosa and Gonaqua Hottentots. This is an interesting story which had its beginning in the practice of Xhosa chiefs of the time of killing off any subject whose herd of cattle was attractively large, under the pretext that he was a witch. The herd was then annexed by the chief. In this particular case, the chief concerned was called Tshiwo, and he had as an executioner a man named Kwane. Kwane had a kinder heart than was normal in people of his calling; often, instead of killing a family when they slept at night, he allowed them to escape. He did, however, take their cattle back to the chief, because his remuneration was a certain proportion of such annexed cattle. Those who had been spared usually found shelter with a tribe of Hottentots known as the Gonaqua and thereafter lived with them and intermarried.

Then it happened, in the course of time and owing to fluctuating fortunes, that Chief Tshiwo himself ended up in need of help against his own enemies. He did not know where to turn but, to his surprise and pleasure, Kwane, the executioner, came to his help. Kwane called in the assistance of all his friends whom he had spared from death, and they, and many of the Hottentots with whom they were living, came to Tshiwo's rescue.

Tshiwo was so grateful that, in recognition, he made Kwane a chief in his own right. His subjects were those whose lives he had originally spared and their Gonaqua Hottentot friends. By this time, however, these Xhosa and Gonaqua had so intermingled that separation was impossible, so a new clan was formed who adopted the Xhosa language and ways, called the Gqunukwebe—subjects of Chief Kwane.

The End of a Colourful Era

And so the Xhosa tribe has moved down the generations, but today it has come to the end of an era and is rapidly going over to the white man's way of life. Its people are moving into towns, to schools and towards Christianity and the tribesmen are rapidly abandoning their attractive red blankets. In this process many of their interesting customs, beliefs and rites are being abandoned but, in the quieter corners of the area in which the core of the tribe lives, the Red Blankets still practise customs and rites which are centuries old.

In the chapters which follow, I have tried to describe the way of life of these people and to record their customs, rites and beliefs in a form which will be readable to the layman and yet, perhaps, be useful to the scholar. The greater part of the research for this book was done in the Ciskei, and the practices described in it are those of the clans in this area. Basic practices are, however, the same throughout the tribe but it does sometimes happen that minor procedures in the execution of rites differ with areas. Yet when it is considered that the Red Blankets are illiterate and that their traditions have been passed down the centuries merely by word of mouth from father to son, it is quite remarkable how generally consistent their beliefs and practices are, in fact, throughout the tribe.

Overleaf from left to right:
A man in typical splendour pauses on his way to visit friends at a neighbouring kraal. The average Xhosa man has tremendous stamina and a fine physique and can walk many miles in the course of a day.

Xhosa women working in the fields.

An elegant, well-dressed woman in true tribal clothes. Unlike girls, married women never go unclad above the waist.

Chapter 2   Life in the Red Blanket Kraal

A group of Xhosa huts of the Ndlambe clan on the road to Kei Mouth. All the doors face the same way, out of the prevailing weather. In the left middle distance is a land of maize, their main crop.

Life in The Red Blanket Kraal

The Red Blanket Xhosa are sociable people, they love the company of their fellow men and keep an open house to any stranger. A traveller, on his way, never has to worry where he will sleep or get the next meal, because any family he comes to will share with him what they have and give him a place by the fire to sleep.

In the same way, when a kraal has a beer-drink or a feast, there is no suggestion of 'who will we ask' because everyone who is near enough is automatically invited, and is expected to stay until there is nothing left of the slaughter to eat and no more beer to drink

The Hut

The family's home is a round mud hut with a pole in the middle supporting a dome-shaped or a conical grass roof. A fire burns in a hollow in the mud plastered floor and, when the weather is too bad to cook outside, a three-legged cast-iron pot stands over it with the next meal slowly cooking inside.

The hut is a simple structure which consists of a basic wall framework made of wattles woven, basket-fashion, in and out of strong stakes let into the ground in a circle. This is plastered over thickly with mud until it is about five inches thick. The floor is made of earth or antheap stamped down hard and smoothed off with mud and finally smeared over with cow dung. The inside of the wall is finished off in the same way and both the wall and the floor are, when a spring clean is necessary, periodically freshened up with a new smear.

The roof framework is made of wattles in the same way as the walls and it is then covered with thatch grass. In some huts, in areas where there is indigenous bush, the Xhosa lace the thatch with a thick wild vine which is found growing over water and is known in those parts as 'monkey rope'. The appearance of the huts in the Ciskei, that is south of the Kei River, is rather untidy compared with those of some of their neighbours like the Thembu and Pondomiese who are north of the river, in the Transkei. The Ciskei Xhosa do not, as a rule, paint any colours or designs on their huts as do the above two tribes but, in the branch of the Xhosa tribe in the Transkei, this is quite common, no doubt as a result of the influence of the neighbouring tribes.

The Xhosa hut has a single door and one tiny wooden window and both are closed tightly at night to keep out witches and the mischievous water sprite called *Tikoloshe*.* Even though the window is too small to allow much to get in, it has to be shut, no matter how hot the weather, because one of the two 'could drop a stone through it on to someone's head while they sleep', or worse still, might blow magic medicine in over the sleeping people and make them sick or bring all kinds of other evil on them.

When a new hut is to be built, all the men and women of the neighbourhood help with the work. The men make the skeleton framework of wattles and the women then take over and with their bare hands, build up the wall with mud. When

---

* This sprite is common to many bantu tribes in the Republic of South Africa but, among some, he is known as *Tokoloshe*.

Left : A girl doing beadwork for her sweetheart.

Right : A social get-together. Men's tobacco bags are always a feature of both their ceremonial and everyday dress. Bags of the type in this picture are made from goat skins which are pulled off the carcase with the minimum of cutting. The clay-painted design on the hut is not a regular feature of Xhosa huts in the Ciskei—the idea is borrowed from neighbouring tribes in the Transkei.

28

A Xhosa hut under construction. Men build the framework and then women take over and build up the mud walls with their bare hands.

Right: The "little" wife paints her face to signify that she is still suckling her baby, while she looks into the mirror in her left hand. She crushes the white clay or chalk on the stone in front of her. The "big" wife, with one of her children watching her, is busy freshening up the inside of her hut with a smear of new cow dung. The headdress of the women on the left, under which she has to lift her head backwards to see ahead, shows that she is still very "unimportant" as a married woman. That of the other indicates that she has gained some status by giving her father-in-law some grandchildren.

this is dry, it is the women who smear out the inside of the wall and floor with cow dung and thereafter keep the inside of the hut in this condition.

Women always cut the thatch grass, and it is a picturesque sight to see them coming home at sundown, walking in single file with long bundles on their heads, silhouetted against the red sun.

Being sociable people, Xhosa families build their huts close together. This custom is second nature now to them but, apart from a desire for each other's company, the custom must have had a much more serious origin in the tribe's old warring days when they relied on the protection that community living offered.

In a group of huts the doors all face the same way to suit the lie of the land and the prevailing winds and rain, and they always face towards the gate of the cattle pen which is built close to the hut, so that the owners can hear if their cattle are disturbed at night. No matter how big the family is, unless there is more than one wife, everyone sleeps in the same hut and this includes any visitors who might be calling.

This is not because of poverty or any expenses that would be involved in building more huts, because material and labour are usually free, but purely because of the custom and usage on the farms in the Ciskei. Most families do, however, usually have an additional small hut which is used as a storeroom. In other areas they often have more huts. At night each one rolls himself or herself up naked in a red ochre-dyed blanket next to the fire. Each one sleeps on his own mat of rushes but very few seem to use anything under their heads except some who use a wooden block which they shape for this purpose.

The Byre

A feature of every Xhosa home is its stock byre or cattle 'kraal'. Every family has one. In the Ciskei where trees are plentiful, most of them are made from the branches of the mimosa (the 'thorn tree') arranged in a circle with the brush of the tree on the inside and the chopped off trunks on the outside. This kraal, or stock pen, is the symbol of the Xhosa home and is built to protect the family's cattle and goats at

The pipemaker. He has a woman's pipe— identified by its long stem—in his mouth, a man's pipe in his hand and the start of a more decorative man's pipe lies between his feet. All pipes have short, removable mouthpieces.

night from marauding dogs, jackals and thieves, as a place to milk the cows and as the place in which the family makes ritual sacrifices to its ancestors and where they carry out various tribal customs.

The word 'kraal' in South Africa is used in a wide sense by both English and Afrikaans speaking people. They use it to denote the cattle pen as described above; the individual family home and, in a more general sense, to mean a community of homes in a group. The Xhosa, themselves, in their own language differentiate quite clearly between the three and 'kraal' is used by them to denote the byre.

Traditional Dress

In the many South African Bantu tribes it is almost invariably the woman who predominates in her traditional dress. In some tribes, today, it would, in fact, be difficult to find a man in tribal clothing. Among the Xhosa, numerically, far more women dress only in their tribal clothes than do their men; but in *splendour* the women would often be hard-pressed to outdo some of their men when the latter turn themselves out in their tribal clothes for special feasts or beer-drinks.

I should explain at this stage that during the week, when they are working, Xhosa men wear the white man's style of clothing because, firstly, it would be too inconvenient to work in blankets and, secondly, because civilisation in all its aspects is spreading fast into even the most remote pockets of the 'raw' Xhosa that remain. But it is in his leisure time that the raw tribesman dresses up. With the women, the picture is different. In the country areas of the Ciskei, when they are not actually working in the white man's home, the common dress of most of the women and girls is the red blanket, whether they are hoeing the mealie lands or going out to the local trader's shop. Then it is on Sundays, days of leisure and at feasts and beer-drinks, that both sexes dress up in their very best tribal outfits.

The basic conventional tribal dress of both the Xhosa man and woman is a red blanket-wrap supplemented, in the case of the woman, with a wide ankle-length skirt which has many rows of black braid around the bottom foot or more of

its length. Married women never appear in public naked from the waist up in the way that young unmarried girls do.

The material used by the women is a white cotton baize which they buy by the yard and make up by hand. The men on the other hand use much heavier, conventional blankets which are white when they buy them. In both cases the cloth is dyed with red ochre before it is used and the depth of red varies from just tinted-white to a deep intense brick-red, according to the custom of their particular clan and to the locality in which they live. White blankets are occasionally seen, but this is not normal as white is reserved for their witch-doctors. Among the Xhosa, white is a symbol of spiritual purity, a 'happy' colour, while black is regarded as an ominous one.

Clothes can be dyed in two ways. Either the dry ochre powder is sprinkled thickly over the material which is then folded and beaten continuously with a stick until the powder filters through it thoroughly; or the ochre is mixed with water and used as a conventional liquid dye.

The head-dress of both men and women is a turban folded so that it stands out in a high, loose, arrangement. These turbans they call '*doeks*', and the popular colours are navy-blue, black, brown and a deep green, but the men occasionally today wear something revolutionary like a tartan. The longer a woman has been married the higher and more elaborately she is entitled to wear her *doek*. Brides start off by wearing theirs tied almost like skull-caps around their heads.

Unlike the women of many other tribes, Xhosa women have no hairstyles at all. Their head decoration is their turban and in public they wear it continuously. In the same way men and the older boys and girls usually keep their heads covered in company. Girls ordinarily wear a small *doek*, but modestly and more closely wrapped and sometimes even a coloured handkerchief. But when they are dressed up in their best beads and miniature red skirts to meet the boys on a Sunday, they often wear beads on their heads instead of *doeks*.

The teenage, or older group of boys have in the past also worn a small *doek* or handkerchief on their heads but today

31

The matmaker. These are the conventional rush mats on which the Xhosa sleep next to the fire on the floor of their huts.

Left: Bringing home the firewood.

are adopting a high cap with a small peak. It is usually a dark colour and is decorated with beads for 'going out'.

It is impossible to tell just how long a Xhosa man or woman's hair would grow if it was given the chance, because they never let it grow longer than about an inch before they shave it off, down to the skull, 'because it is too hot'. They believe that human hair is one of the most dangerous 'medicines' there is for a witch to get hold of because he can use it in magic mixtures to cast all kinds of spells over its owner. Furthermore, if a witch finds a girl's hair he can make a powerful love-potion with it which he can sell for a high price to any young man who wants to win her love.

For this reason, when the Xhosa cut their hair, they guard every visible piece of it, so that the birds cannot take it off to their nests where witches will find it. Then, when no one is around to see them, they take the hair and bury it under the brush of the cattle kraal.

Beads, Pipes and Smoking

On ceremonial occasions, like feasts, beer-drinks or even Sunday visits to their neighbours, both men and women wear beads in profusion, though a well-dressed man carries a greater number and more varied pieces than his wife does. A married woman's beads are mostly confined to broad, flat, necklaces of many colours, some wrist or arm pieces and a few strings around her ankles. She also wears necklaces of cow tail hair or of roots, or even bones, for magic protection and healing.

In addition, she often wears a series of narrow brass bands from her wrists to her elbows. Each band is about an eighth of an inch wide and fits so closely to the next that the flesh does not show between them. As a woman gets older and puts on weight so the bands get tighter and start to hurt and irritate and the only way she gets any relief at all, and that is very little, is to rub the one metal arm against the other. She cannot get under the bands to scratch. I remember, as a child, that we had a particularly fine old domestic servant whose name was Annie Noseven who, we understood, had royal blood in her veins, having descended from a line of

chiefs. Her arms were heavily plated in this way and she suffered agony, with her flesh bulging at each end of the bands but, despite all our persuasion she would not take them off. She said it was the custom of her family and that it would upset the spirits of her forefathers if she were to do so and, if they were unhappy, they might make her sick or bring some other evil on her.

The man's beads are a work of art and they exhibit the untiring patience of the artists who make them. One of the finest collections of man's beads that I have seen is that of a man named Dumane in the Kei Road area. He has seventy-two pieces, each of which has its own name like the 'tie', the 'belt' and the 'anklet', and some of them are so large that they literally contain many thousands of individual beads. The collection is so heavy that Dumane only wears all the pieces at one time when he has a beer-drinking party at his own home and at Christmas time, because he 'cannot otherwise walk very far with them.'

The type of bead used by the Xhosa is the very smallest available in the trading stores and the colours most used are white, blue, red and pink. The overall effect of a finished piece of Xhosa beadwork is modest and even delicate in colouring, compared with the strong colours of the heavier beads I have seen, among some of the Zulu tribes.

Among the Xhosa, the pieces worn by each age group of both sexes differ quite clearly and, strangely enough, the girls do not as a rule wear anything like the quantity, or quality of pieces of beads that their boy friends do. Brides wear very little because they are relatively unimportant before they have borne children. Young mothers, apart from a few necklaces of magical significance, do not wear much more. As married women grow in status they wear more and increasingly elaborate necklaces but not a large variety of pieces.

The beads of a tribe are a study in themselves and many pieces have specific meanings and convey messages from the wearer. For instance, a girl's necklace in a certain pattern and in particular colours might mean that she has a sweetheart. Then, as a counterpart to this, she might give her boy

friend a necklace in which she sets out her message of love.

All beadwork is done by the women and girls of a kraal. Married women make the pieces which they and their husbands wear and girls work for their brothers, for themselves and for their sweethearts. That girls have so much work to do for others possibly accounts for the fact that they do not generally wear more beads themselves.

Both Xhosa men and women smoke pipes and their 'tobacco bags' are decorative additions to their outfits. The woman's is made of white cotton baize and is about nine inches wide and twelve to fifteen inches long from the mouth to the bottom. It hangs by a cotton baize strap over the shoulder and rests on the wearer's hip on the opposite side. It is decorated with small patterns of beadwork, rows of black braid and such things as little jingling bells and a tassel or two of red or green wool. In the bag the woman carries her supply of dried home-grown tobacco leaves; a small round hand-mirror with a red celluloid back; her pipe with a foot long stem and a three inch high bowl; a tin of snuff and a small lady's handkerchief in the corner of which

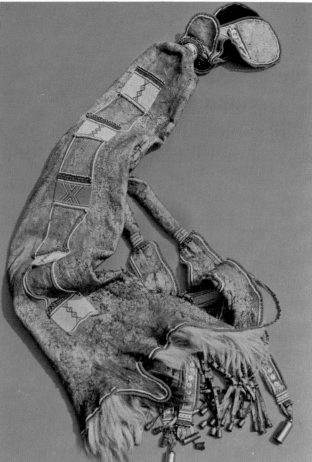

tied in a knot, is her shopping money.

The man's bag is quite different and more masculine. It is made from a wild or domestic animal's skin. The particular skin used, to some extent, owes its popularity to the fashion in a clan in the same way as does the pattern by which it is made up. In the Ncera area, near Kidd's Beach, where I lived as a child, the popular bag was a tubular one made of monkey skin. In other areas goat skins are used for this purpose. These bags have always fascinated me, particularly because of the ingenuity with which the monkey or goat is skinned. The carcase is simply taken out of its skin to leave the skin nearly intact in its origional shape but without an animal inside it. To do this, they first cut the animal's feet off or, in the case of a monkey, its feet and hands. Then they slit the skin from under the chin lengthwise down the throat to the chest where they stop. With this starting point, they skin the head and neck up and backwards towards the shoulders. After this they 'loosen' the next area of skin ahead by forcing their hands in between the skin and the flesh. Thereafter the skin separated from the forequarters is carefully pulled inside out and backwards until, with a great deal of patience, the whole skin is removed from the carcase intact.

The skin is now sun-dried and cured at the river without removing the hair. To make the tobacco bag the skin is turned inside out with the hair inside, the legs and neck are tied off with laces of leather and the mouth of the bag is made at the tail end. To complete the process the bag is decorated with beads and tassels and odds and ends, and a leather strap is fitted to it so that it can be slung from the shoulder. Some of the goat skin bags made in this fashion are often three feet long and are so ornamental that they are carried as show-pieces over the arm when the owner goes out visiting. Inside the bag, the man is likely to have the same things as the woman does plus, always, a pocket-knife and a sharp spike

for taking thorns out of his feet. This spike which is usually sheathed in a length of wood, is necessary because the country Xhosa's traditional means of transport is his own bare feet and in traversing the paths across the rough veld he gets many thorns in them.

A type of man's bag which is popular in the Cove Rock (Gompo) locality near East London is one made from the skin of the wild spotted Genet cat. This bag is quite different from the monkey skin bag. It is flat and is in the rough shape of the opened out skin. It is made by sewing two skins together down the outside edges with the seam turned inwards and the hair, this time, on the outside. One of the tails is left to dangle as an ornament and the skin of one of the heads is used as a flap over the mouth of the bag. Again, the bag is sus-

Below: Young wives, with their headdress signifying that they are relatively newly married, hoeing the maize field of one of their husbands. Xhosa people help each other in most family duties.

Opposite: Lolombela Mbangeli reminiscing at Cove Rock. His people regard shellfish as a delicacy and their womenfolk are frequently seen at low tide searching the rocks for mussels and other shellfish. His tobacco bag made of the skins of a wild genet cat is typical of the members of his clan, the Gqunukwebe.

pended from the shoulder and hangs against the wearer's hip.

Smoking is part of the social life of the Xhosa and, whenever men and women meet with any time at all to spare, they bring out their pipes and whoever has tobacco in his bag shares it with the rest. To light his pipe, the Xhosa man picks up a glowing coal out of the fire quite casually with his fingers and, without hurrying, shakes it backwards and forwards in his cupped hand a few times so that it is never in one place long enough to burn him and then puts it on top of the tobacco in his pipe. Women do the same just as easily.

A habit that both sexes have while smoking is that of spitting. It is almost an automatic part of their smoking routine to shape their tongue behind nearly clenched teeth and send a sharp jet of saliva through them to land yards away on the ground or hut floor.

If the tobacco is not brought out by whoever has it when friends meet then someone will openly ask 'who has got tobacco?' The Xhosa are never modest about this, and they have a stock phrase which they use when they meet anyone, white or black, who they think might 'fill their pipes'.

Gifts

Tobacco is the traditional present to give a Xhosa man or woman and white farmers in the Ciskei have a habit of saying to their employees, when they give them a *bhasela** (present) of *cash,* 'Here you are, buy tobacco'. Such gifts, no matter how small, are gratefully and graciously received, and as a token of respect in taking them the Xhosa always hold out both hands (the one resting in the other) to the giver. Just as they show respect in receiving a present, they also expect dignity in the giver in giving, and they regard it as an insult to have money thrown to them or dropped at their feet. It would be quite common for a Xhosa to disdain and ignore a present from anyone inexperienced or thoughtless enough to give it to him in this way. He would walk away and leave it where it had dropped.

The Red Blanket Xhosa is a simple, and good person. He

---

* The 'h' is silent.

is tremendously appreciative of kindness and I can remember numerous occasions when, as a child, I was brought a present of a fowl or even a pumpkin by one of my father's old servants as a token of appreciation for some little thing I might have done for one of his or her family. No matter how little they can afford it, they show their appreciation in some way, even if it is only to give a cob or two of green mealies from their garden. Often, when they borrowed a few shillings from my father or mother we would hear nothing more about it for perhaps a year when quite unexpectedly they would appear with the repayment and their warm expressions of gratitude for the 'kindness they had been shown'.

Duties and Etiquette in the Homestead

The Xhosa *man* is master of his home and no one is ever left in any doubt of this fact. Occasionally a strong woman emerges and dominates the family and her husband, but this is not common and when it does happen, it is usually the result of a weak man having a strong-willed wife. The father is the head of the family and its spiritual leader on earth and, when he passes on, he guides and influences them 'from the place to which he has gone'.

In the home, the father and his sons are the keepers of the cattle and other livestock—these are the wealth of the family—while the mother and her daughters take care of all the domestic duties. The men sow the mealie and kaffircorn (*sorghum*) lands, but the womenfolk hoe them and keep them clear of weeds. The women gather wood for the fires; carry water, cook and sew, and the girls are the nursemaids. The girls are also expected to help their mothers in whatever else they can around the home. Both wives and daughters have to obey the head of the family in all that he tells them or suffer the possible penalty of a hiding if they upset him.

Xhosa women carry any and everything on their heads. They can balance loads of all shapes, sizes and weights with little outward effort whether it is a bottle of paraffin from the trading store; a four gallon bucket of water or even a hundred or more pounds of mealies in a grain bag. A result of walking with loads balanced in this way is that all the

37

This girl's entire outfit is made of tiny white beads. It is the only one of its type I have seen.

Centre: A boy before his initiation to manhood.

Far right: This picture of two boys on their way to a Sunday gathering was captured only three miles from the City of East London. The rattles on their legs could be heard for a considerable distance as the boys jogtrotted along.

women in the tribe have a graceful erect deportment. Men do not carry any loads when they go out with their wives. The reason for this is that they are the traditional defenders of the party and all they carry are one or two fighting sticks, usually across the back of the shoulders.

Xhosa boys are brought up strictly and they know full well what will happen to them if they let the cattle stray into the crops. Their penalty is a thrashing.

Just as men rule in the home so, too, on ceremonial occasions like sacrifices and feasts, or at beer-drinks, they predominate. They are the heads. Strict etiquette is followed on these occasions by both sexes and each age group. Married men sit on the ground near the gate of the cattle byre, married women stay apart at a distance from the men; young brides keep themselves in the background somewhere else; boys play at a respectful distance and the girls keep close by them.

I should, perhaps, explain here for the sake of clarity that 'boys' are those males who have not been through the initiation to manhood ceremony of circumcision. The uneducated, Red Blanket Xhosa, have no knowledge of their own age in years, but this ceremony takes place at about the time when a male is in his late teens or early twenties. Without it, if he dies at ninety, he is still a 'boy' and a 'thing' without any status or seniority in the tribe.

For their feasts the Xhosa slaughter oxen or goats depending on the occasion. They make beer by the forty-four gallon drum and boil up pots full of dry mealies *(maize)* to eat. The time chosen for a feast is almost invariably a week-end and the guests start arriving for it on the Saturday morning. After that the party goes on non-stop all afternoon, throughout Saturday night and all Sunday until the meat and other food is eaten up and there is no beer left. Then the thick-headed, noisy, contented guests start weaving their various unsteady ways out into the darkness in the direction of home. Many are not behind the plough the next day and others are so lethargic that they may as well have stayed at home, like their friends, and pretended to be sick.

Kaffir Beer

The tribal beer which the Xhosa make, and which the white people call 'Kaffir beer', is made from maize or kaffir corn.

The long skirt of this girl signifies that she is in the group of a "young man's girl" – a "boy's girl" would wear a short skirt. The fold of her headdress shows that she is not married. She has been cutting thatch grass for the family hut with the sickle.

The dry grain is soaked in water for twenty-four hours then spread out, sandwiched between two wet hessian grain bags until it sprouts. But before the little shoots start turning green the grain is spread out in the sun to dry again. The shoots lose their fatness and shrivel. The grain is then ready to mill into meal. The women do this by putting the grain a little at a time into the hollow of a concave stone and grinding it with another small oval stone which they can just hold comfortably in their hands.

There is sometimes a variation in the way in which beer is brewed. I have seen the meal, once it is sufficiently fine, put into a container of boiling water and left for a day or two, or for as long as it needs in the temperature at the time, to ferment. By that time the mixture is the consistency of a thin porridge, and it is then boiled over the fire for about two hours and again left to ferment for a few days. After this, the roughage is strained off and what remains is beer ready to drink. It is reputed to be a good health-giving brew.

For strainers the Xhosa, in common with other tribes, traditionally use long funnels two or three feet long made of plaited grass or palm or reed leaves.

Even after it is strained, 'Kaffir beer' is still thick and heavy, yet a man or woman thinks nothing of sitting down to half a gallon or a gallon of it at a time. And, over the period of a feast, they can drink almost unbelievable quantities of it. The sociable way in which they drink their beer is to sit around in a circle on the grass – in the respective adult groups which etiquette demands – and pass a canful around from person to person. At the same time a pipe does the rounds of the group for each to have a draw in their turn.

The national drink of the tribe is their beer; sometimes they buy brandy which they drink neat. When a man comes home with a bottle he drinks it in one sitting with his friends. The host fills a measure for each person in turn. The drinker in silence, watched by everyone, puts his head back and downs the neat drink in a single gulp. Then with a 'haaa!' of satisfaction, which also helps to cool his throat, he passes the empty measure back and wipes his mouth with the back of his hand.

Mentality, Outlook and Beliefs

The Supreme Architect made of the Xhosa a proud, but carefree and happy people. They adapt themselves to whatever fortunes come their way; they are grateful for the good and do not fret over the bad. Time to them is unimportant, they live for the moment they are in. At night, stories are told about all the events of the day and soon thereafter when it is dark, everyone curls up and goes to sleep. They get up with the dawn. But young boys and girls, on the other hand, can just as easily dance and sing throughout a night and half the next day.

In their old tradition, the Xhosa were hunters and herdsmen and their migrations of the past have been largely in the tracks of wild game and in search of better grazing for their cattle. Today, they are still a pastoral people with their cattle and sheep and goats, while dogs and fowls are a feature of most homes. In their lands they plant mealies, kaffir corn, melons, pumpkins and, always, tobacco.

The Red Blanket Xhosa is today still happiest when he is nearest to nature. He looks to the white man for guidance, protection and care, he marvels over the white man's inventions and 'flying machines' and calls them 'the things of the white man'; but his own tempo of life is still slow and he likes it that way. To jolt him out of it overnight would be to throw him into a millstream completely unprepared to look after himself. The Xhosa despise weakness of character but admire and respect strength. Their old chiefs ruled them with a strong hand and today discipline is ingrained in them, it is part of their way of life. It is evident in all facets of their daily existence and it is perhaps most clearly seen in the home where the father's word is unquestioned and obeyed.

The Red Blanket Xhosa are pagans and pay homage to the spirits of their ancestors. They are known as the 'raw ones' and many of their ideas and beliefs must in many respects still be the same today as they were when the Xhosa met the white man some three centuries ago. Their beliefs are fascinating in their simplicity and unique, so that one feels that the Xhosa live in a spiritual world quite apart. To understand the Xhosa, one must understand and accept the way

Above: Girls are trained from an early age to help their mothers with the domestic duties in the family.

Below: Loaded shoppers returning home from the trading store. Women carry all their luggage on their heads whether it is a bottle of paraffin, a cabbage or a hundred pounds of maize in a sack.

their minds work; one should never ridicule their beliefs but instead should let one's mind have full reign in this Xhosa world of imagination and see the things that they see there. In this way one finds that there is a meaning in their cult. It is something very clearly defined to those who believe in it. It is a cult far removed from the modern world and the Red Blanket Xhosa – like most uneducated bantu – live by a code of spiritual rules. During the week they go about their work, whatever it may be in the civilised world, but the moment that anything goes wrong in their homes, whether it is sickness or cattle loss or crop failure, they turn inwards to magic.

I mentioned, at the beginning of this chapter, the sociable habits of the Red Blankets and how they share what they have and how a feast is for everyone. In the same way, trouble is everybody's concern, sickness is the work of the witches and, where witches are, the community stands together to get rid of them. And there is only one way of fighting a witch's magic and that is with greater magic – that of the witch-doctor. If anyone is sick or something is lost, the cause is supernatural and so all who are able must get together and go off to consult the nearest or best witch-doctor. He is a *diviner* and smells out, by communing with the spirits, who is casting the evil over the homestead and causing trouble. They, the spirits, tell him, the doctor, who is to blame and he in turn passes the information on to the all-believing audience.

Xhosa magic takes many forms and these are discussed in detail later, but it seems appropriate to mention here one or two of their beliefs and ideas to give the reader an early insight into their minds and the ways in which they reason.

The mysteries of their spiritual world find expression in their reasoning and, just as magic is used by witches to create evil, so stronger magic is used to remedy the ill. But witches and witch-doctors are not the only people who use magic for, in everyday life, private individuals get mixed up in various ways in the practice of magic. An example that has always fascinated me is the ritual of rain-making by an ordinary man. This operation is kept secret by the person doing it because, if he lets the weather get out of control and he brings floods, then he will be beaten by the other men of the kraal, and he might even be chased out until the rain stops.

To make rain the person must trap a big brown bird which the Xhosa call a *Thekwane** (a hammerkop). It always lives near the water and is hard to catch, especially when it has to be caught secretly. It is killed and thin wire is tied around its legs to hang it head-down from a branch over the river bed. This particular part of the operation can cause all the trouble because, when the river fills, the water will come up to wherever the bird is and if it has been hung too high there will, because of this, be floods.

Worse will happen if the bird is carried away with the water because then the rain will go on for weeks with nothing to stop it. That is why it is hung up with *wire*.

The Xhosa have interesting little beliefs, too, about many normal occurrences; for example, they say about the picking-up of money: 'you must buy with it something to eat, then your eyes will be made sharp to pick up more money!'

Their theory on dog bites is surprising in that they literally believe in 'the hair of the dog that bit you . . .' How, when and where their theory originated would be difficult to say, but I encountered an actual example of their treatment for dog bites while doing research for this book. A family in the Kidd's Beach area, about twenty-five miles from East London, sent one of their young piccanins along to the trading store for some goods and the child was bitten by a white man's dog. Unfortunately the incident took place without the owner's knowledge and the child went home crying. The next morning before the sun was up, a member of the child's family was back to see the dog's owner. He said the child had not slept all night and its father wanted some of the dog's hair to put in the wound. The owner's offer of medical treatment was refused and it was explained that they would burn the hair and rub the cinders into the bite and that this would heal the wound, but if they did not do this, the child would never get well.

---

* The 'h' is silent.

Chapter 3   The Man, His Marriage and His Home

A girl hoeing the pineapple fields. The hessian skirt is to protect her from the thorny leaves of the plants.

Right: The Xhosa are sociable people and build their homes together in groups and a community of this kind is commonly referred to as a Kraal.

By tradition the Xhosa man is the undisputed head of his home and the master of his family. When he goes out with his wife he walks in front and she follows five or six paces behind with her baby on her back and their luggage on her head. If he has more than one wife they follow behind each other in order of seniority. Among commoners, the first wife is the main or great wife but among chiefs this is not so; instead she is regarded as an inferior wife, or the wife who was taken in the young man's inexperience and as the experiment of his youth.

Marriage in the tribe is by arrangement. It is not an affair of the heart and is not traditionally the culmination of courtship. Romance comes into the picture only in exceptional cases and love is not a pre-requisite to a union. It is not even a consideration in the true tribal marriage ceremony that has been passed down through the centuries.

The Xhosa are polygamous and their men may have as many wives as they can afford to acquire under the *lobolo* system, which entails the payment of cattle to the bride's father.

This should not be interpreted to mean that all men have several wives. Far from it. Marriage is too costly a business among the Xhosa for that, and the man with more than one wife is the exception rather than the rule. The influence of civilisation is also having its effect and the more enlightened among the Xhosa are turning to the white man's ways, so that the polygamists in the tribe today are almost entirely among the 'raw' tribesmen.

Lobolo*

Marriage is an expensive business by the standards of the uneducated tribesmen because most fathers ask a marriage payment of anything from seven to fourteen head of cattle for their daughters. In cash this would be something like R300 or about £150 upwards. If the cattle are of a good quality the currency equivalent would, of course, be a lot higher but the Red Blankets, like all uneducated bantu, are much more impressed by quantity, and the bridegroom can usually get away with some young cattle and others of indifferent breeding in the total he offers.

Fortunately payment of the *lobolo* by *instalments* is accepted in the tribe and, provided the bridegroom can raise a certain proportion of the stock at the beginning, he is allowed to take his bride and pay the rest as he earns. Sometimes this takes him all his life and it even happens that when his sons grow up they have to help him pay the *lobolo* for their mother.

The young man knows that after his initiation to manhood, his next step is marriage and to get the necessary money quickly he usually leaves his home in the country and goes away to work on the gold mines for a year or more. The money he can save there gives him a good start, after which he returns to his home kraal ready to look around for a wife.

Sentiment is not supposed to come into a man's choice of a partner and, in fact, it would be frowned upon if he were to carry off his boyhood sweetheart as a bride, though occasionally some young couples are clever enough to hood-

---

* *Lobolo* is the noun, e.g. the payment of *lobolo*. *Lobola* is the verb, e.g. to take a wife.

42

wink their parents and end up together. An interesting example of the Xhosa routine in marriage came to my notice when I was in the Kei Road Area of the Ciskei. A middle aged man had lost his first wife a year before and his friends were insisting that he should take another. There was no one in his neighbourhood whose qualifications suited him so he sent a messenger to one of his relatives living twenty or thirty miles away towards the coast and asked them to please look around for a new wife for him. When last I saw the man he said that his uncle, the relative, had not yet found anyone 'but he *would*, because he knew many people'.*

Ideas on the suitability of a bride are based largely on a girl's capability and energy. Looks are not very important to the average man but he likes his wife to be buxom, strong and able to work hard, and also considered fit to bear many children because fertility is regarded as a gift of great goodness.

When a man has found the girl whom he wishes to take as his wife, he sends an ambassador to her father to negotiate for him. He does not go himself. If the father is satisfied to let his daughter go to the man and to the family concerned then he talks business and the question of the *lobolo* is discussed in detail, but before this stage is reached the girl's mother is consulted. This is one of the few instances in Xhosa womanhood where the woman has any authority or, in fact, where she has the last say, because only if she is satisfied with the

---

* I eventually returned to this Kei Road scene when the *Magic World of the Xhosa* was already in the hands of the printers and enquired about subsequent developments in the drama. The story was tragic. James (the name of the man) had, in the end, found *himself* a new wife and within a year had a child. This resulted in a great deal of satisfaction in his home but then, unaccountably to their way of thinking, in a short while it became ill and died. The father was not only distraught but alarmed and went to his farmer employer to ask if he could have some time off to take the members of his kraal to a witch-doctor to 'smell out' the witch who had caused this. It was obvious, he said, that someone was bewitching them. Feeling it his duty, the farmer reasoned with the man and eventually discouraged him from going, but it is doubtful whether he convinced him that to refrain was wise.

After some months the young wife again became expectant but this time she and James decided that she would go to her parents' home and have the child there, where she would be away from the immediate influence of the witch in their own midst. At the end of her time the woman gave birth not to one child, but to twins. Again tragedy struck and one of them died. Panic-stricken, the mother brought

man who wants to carry off her child, will the marriage go through. If the mother gives her consent then her husband and the bridegroom's ambassador start bargaining. The father sets a *lobolo* according to his idea of her popularity in the marriage market. If the girl is intelligent and industrious and likely to be sought after then he aims high. But if he is uncertain and feels that she might be left on the shelf, then he is more reasonable and settles for a fair amount rather than lose the proverbial 'bird in the hand'.

The marriage payment is not always only in cattle but sometimes includes a few white goats or even a horse.

With the advance of civilisation amongst the Xhosa, an increasing number of marriages today are more 'enlightened' and the girl knows of her impending marriage and, in the Transkei in particular, actually takes her part in a public ceremony which includes dancing, the slaughter of cattle and feasting. But, on the farms and in the reserves in the Ciskei a large proportion of the marriages are still on the *thwala* (carry) basis where the bride is physically carried off by her future husband.

Under this system, once the marriage payment is agreed upon, a date is fixed unknown to the bride-to-be, and plans are made between the father and the husband's representative for the abduction. Then, at the time agreed, the father sends his daughter out on some errand, perhaps to fetch water or

the other baby back to James and her own home, but it was not long before the second child died as well. Fears ran high and suspicion built up, not only in the minds of James and his wife, but in those of all the Xhosa on the farm . . . *who* was the witch in their midst? They knew their master did not agree with them about the advisability of getting in a witch-doctor, and so they settled down in a state of uneasy acceptance of their fate.

Then one day the young wife nervously approached their employer, the farmer, when none of the other servants were around and, as a child would, told him that 'she was frightened'. James, she said, wanted to sleep with her again, but how could she allow it when she knew she 'had something wrong inside' because someone had used magic medicine on her?

Sympathetically, and with the understanding that was so necessary, her employer reminded her how, among all the creatures around them, events like this happened all the time. This was nature. The cows lost their calves, the sheep their lambs and the goats their kids—this was the way of all life, he told her.

The next day the woman ran away and James was once again alone.

wood, to a place where the husband-to-be and three or four other young men who are his retinue, wait for her. As she comes along either by herself or accompanied by her friends, the young men casually engage her in light conversation because this is customary among the Xhosa who never pass each other without a chat. Then the leader of the young men bluntly tells her she is to be carried off. His assistants, but not the husband himself, roughly grab her. She screams, scratches, bites and laments and struggles quite hysterically to get loose. If she refuses to come of her own accord, they drag or carry her away without any suggestion of respect or

Left: A young beau watches the next meal being prepared.

The long skirt of the girl on the left, who is doing a dance, denotes that she is of marriageable age. She is a "young man's girl". The style of his cap and the paucity of his clothing tells that the third in the group is a boy who has not yet been through the Abakwetha ceremony. His left hand is protected for fighting.

45

Left: A fine collection of beadwork in which the pieces worn by the men predominate. The beaded stick held by the girl on the left is interesting in that items of this nature are not normally seen among the Xhosa.

Right: The unwitting "bride" and two of her friends are waylaid on the road by her future husband (at extreme right) and his "bride-grooms". After engaging her in light conversation to disarm her, the male assistants then surround her and take her away by force to the hut of her husband-to-be.

Below right: The bride is dragged into her "kidnapper"-husband's home by his assistants while he, on the right, casually stands by and watches.

The marriage ceremony: the bride is carried off, while the bridegroom picks up clothing that she has dropped in the struggle.

sympathy for a weaker sex—that is, if she is of the weaker sex because the strength and violence she exhibits is certainly no evidence of it. But in spite of all her struggling she has little hope of escape and ends up at her man's home.

Sometimes these *thwala* ceremonies take place at night. Frequently, as a child on my father's farm, I heard loud screaming and wailing in the dark hours and the next morning I would be told by one of our Xhosa servants that so and so had been 'carried off last night'.

While the girl is being dragged along she sheds bits and pieces of clothing and, though the man who is to be her husband follows behind and picks them up, he takes no other physical part in her kidnapping. When the party gets to the hut which will be the couple's home, the bridegroom drops the clothing he has collected at her feet. This indicates to her that he, among the abductors, is the one who is to be her husband.

The husband's home is not always his own hut and, in fact, if he is taking his first wife, more likely than not it will be that of his parents.

Hlonipha—The Payment of Respect

At the kraal, the womenfolk take over. The bride, or the *umtshakazi* as she is called, is taken inside and stripped of her beads and girl's clothing and from this time on, she will never again go around in public naked above her waist. The women smear her from head to toe with a red paste made from powdered ochre and dress her in the style of a bride which is quite different from that of both girls and married women. These are the symbols of a bride and she has to go about painted in this fashion until after her first child is born. Her red blankets are now draped in their own particular style and a black cloth (*doek* or *iqhiya*) is wrapped tightly around her head to come down over her forehead and so low over her eyes that she has to tilt her head backwards to see. This *doek* is one of the many signs of respect, known as *hlonipha*, which a bride has to show to her father-in-law. Another *hlonipha* requirement is that, from now on, she may

never again say his name or use any word in which the first syllable is the same as in the first syllable of his name. Furthermore, she has also to respect the names of her husband's father and grandfathers as far back as they can be remembered. In the same way her new husband for his part has to *hlonipha* (pay respect to) his wife's mother and her female predecessors. The husband also pays respect to his mother-in-law when he goes to visit her home by carrying his stick (knobkerrie) with the top down and almost on the ground. This is a stick of peace and not the fighting stick which it is when carried in the traditional head-up style or across the back of the shoulders. Another time when the man carries his stick down is when he goes to ask for work. It is a token of subservience. His stick, which is four to five feet long, in fact has only a very small knob. The Xhosa man takes it wherever he goes.

When the woman refers to her father-in-law, she has to call him the 'father of . . .' (his eldest son, but if that son is her husband, she has to use yet another substitute name for the husband). In cases where she has to evade some other word because it has the same first syllable as the name of her father-in-law, she gets around the difficulty by substituting a synonym or the name of a substitute commodity. In addition, women also build up a collection of words of their own— or their mothers-in-law compile the list for them—which they use as substitutes for the prohibited words. The complications of this system will be appreciated when it is considered that the people using it are illiterate and have to memorise the words because they cannot write them down. The effect is that the bride has to know her list off by heart and her audience has to sort out and understand what she is talking about.

If the young woman in her carelessness does say the father-in-law's name, it is a very serious matter; first, she has to hide from him and then return home to her parents for a present for him from her father. In these days, the present demanded is a bottle or two of brandy and the bride is not allowed to eat in her father-in-law's hut until she has brought it. Perhaps the most difficult of the prohibitions placed on the bride is that she is never allowed to call her own husband by his name. She addresses him as the 'brother of' so and so or, if he has no brother, she calls him by some other improvised name.

After her arrival at her man's hut (Xhosa women literally refer to their husbands as 'my man' and men to their wives as 'my woman', as they have no individual words in everyday use meaning 'husband' or 'wife'), and after she has been painted red and re-dressed, the bride is taken outside by the women of the community and instructed in her duties as a wife. This takes the form of a mock demonstration of how to use a hoe and how she must carry wood on her head for the fire and then, of particular importance, she is given a water bucket and made to go through the routine she has to follow when fetching water from the nearest pool for the hut. There is a strict rule attached to the bride carrying water in that when she comes out of the hut she has to turn right and go around the back of the hut. She is not allowed to leave the hut to the left because that is the way her husband goes. When she returns with the water she follows the same route. This law must be obeyed until she has had her first baby, whereafter she is allowed to relax it. If she is slow in having a child she stops the practice after some other girl who was married about the same time as she was has had one.

The first year is a difficult one for a young wife. She must adapt herself to a man whom she might never have seen in her life and, from carefree, happy-go-lucky girlhood, she has to grow into a woman and learn to be a serious, subservient wife. Her whole attitude until she has had a baby must be one of quiet, respectful dignity. In older married company she sits to one side and never pushes herself forward because she is only of minor status as a married woman.

After he first child is born she becomes more important. Then she no longer paints herself red and she raises the black head-dress from off her eyes, because she can now look her father-in-law in the eye after having brought him a grand-child. It is only after she has had more children and grown in seniority that she can wear the high turban, so spectacular among the older Xhosa women.

The Bride's Escape

If the husband has any doubts as to whether his new bride will stay, he locks her up. The first week or so is the most dangerous period for him since, if she intends running away, this is when she is most likely to try it. Fortunately for the husband, the girl's father is on his side because, if all efforts fail to keep her in her new home he, the father, has to return the *lobolo*. This worries him not only because he has to give the cattle back but because if, in the same way, she subsequently runs away from another husband her chances in the matrimonial market will be poor and other men will hesitate before taking a chance on her. Where a girl runs away three times her husband usually leaves her and claims his *lobolo* back.

Another risk the husband has to guard against in the first days of married life is an attempt by any lover his bride may have had at the time of her abduction to steal her away from him. If he is caught doing this he may well have to fight his way out and he could easily end up with a cracked skull as Xhosa men always fight with their knobkerries. If, on the other hand, the lover is successful in getting her away, then he goes to the girl's father and parleys with him over *lobolo* for the girl. If he is able to better that paid by the first man and so satisfy her father and mother of his goodwill and credentials, then it would be in conformity with tribal custom for the parents to agree to his bid. In such a case, the first man has to be given back any cattle he has already delivered.

In most cases, however, the bride does stay with her abductor unless she has a stubborn, determined streak in her character and a strong will of her own. Basically, though, the tradition of her people is so strong that she accepts her fate – this is the Xhosa way of marriage and she must obey. She knows no other way.

One of the first duties of the bride's in-laws is to give her a new name. This is done by the male members of the family but with the mother-in-law also having a say. The name chosen is usually prefixed with 'No' pronounced 'Noh'. This prefix means 'mother of' and has been passed down through untold generations as the 'handle' to a woman's name. The

Above left: The head of the family coming home with his wife who follows respectfully several paces behind. As defender of the party he carries only his fighting stick.

Below left: In her new bridal outfit and painted ochre red, the bride is given a bucket and told how, when going to fetch water at the pool, she has to go around the left side of the hut (as it is faced). This is a sign of respect. She may not go around the right side "because that is the way her husband goes".

Opposite: A Xhosa kraal or community in the Ciskei. The Xhosa are traditionally a farming people and even today they still gauge a family's wealth by its livestock. In the background, behind the discarded hut, is a field of maize, which with meat and milk forms the staple diet of the tribe.

type of name they give their woman is: Nozembe (*Zembe* means 'axe'); Nomanzi (*Manzi* means water) and Nonyanga (*Nyanga* means moon).

A bride, like all Xhosa women, has to work hard and she has to accept her position in the home of her parents-in-law where there are specific rules to obey. One that she has to remember is that the left side of the hut, on entering, belongs to the head of the kraal (her father-in-law) and the right side to her mother-in-law. She and her husband have to share the right side with the latter. If the newly-weds want to be alone at night they take their blankets and go out and sleep in the bushes or else in the small hut which is the family storeroom.

At a later stage, when the husband feels that the time has come, he builds a hut of his own with the help of the other men and women of the community.

If a married woman fails in her duties as a wife or if she displeases her husband in any way she runs the risk of being punished with a hiding. In the same way, for running away from home she might be beaten to teach her a lesson. The husband on his part, however, has to be careful in that if she runs back to her family *because* she has been beaten then her father is entitled to keep her and only release her after he is paid a penalty in cattle. This is one of the features about the *lobolo* system which is aimed at protecting the woman and is in its favour. *Lobolo* is also considered to be an influence in keeping divorces among the Xhosa down to a minimum by reason of the necessity of returning the *lobolo* to an aggrieved husband or on the other hand for the husband having to pay maintenance to his father-in-law if he deserts his wife and she goes home to her parents.

The Cow of the Home

One of the few things a bride contributes to her new home is the 'cow of the home' which her father gives her on her marriage. Every married woman has such a cow and its purpose is to provide hairs from its tail for magic necklaces for its owner. The hairs are plucked from the cow's tail (they may not be cut), in the early light of day and they are bound

into necklaces which fan out around the wearer's neck and give her strong magic protection against sickness and keep away evil spirits.

The cow of the home is never sold and must stay with its owner all its life. Its calves, too, are her property and not that of her husband. When the original cow gets old, one of its heifer calves is set aside to take her place. Then the old animal is killed and eaten by the family and their guests on the same day. Its bones are burned to ashes.

'Hairs of the brush' are worn by the other members of a family at various times also but theirs are taken from a similar cow owned by the head of the family and not by his wife. Her cow is for her use only but his has wider powers and its hair is used for all the children.

Polygamy

Xhosa law allows a Xhosa man to have as many wives as he likes so long as he can afford to pay the *lobolo* for them and the white man's law in South Africa has not interfered with this tribal custom.

In some Xhosa families multiple wives is a tradition and the heir always has more than one. A particular example of this system was found by the author to be practised by Dumane who, with his two wives named Nolindele and Nolisten, lives and works on the same farm as Dumane's father and his two wives.

As mentioned at the beginning of this chapter the first-taken wife of a commoner is his 'great' wife. His subsequent wives rate in seniority in the order in which he married them. The second is his right-hand wife, the third his 'wife of the minor house' attached to the 'great house' and so on, with the further wives rated as minor wives each attached to the two first, or main houses.

The various wives of a single husband, outwardly at least, regard their position as something quite natural. To them it is their peoples' custom and the way of their tribe—so who are they to question it? Among them, tradition, tribal laws and customs are things centuries old. For this reason the husband's right is an established fact and so is the woman's position in life. If she happens to be one of the several wives of the same man she accepts her position, just as does the single wife of another man.

One of the specific remedies used by a polygamous husband to avoid jealousy among his wives is to have a separate hut for each of them. Then, instead of showing favour to any particular woman, he rotates around the huts and spends a certain number of nights with each of them.

In addition to his wife, or wives, a man often has a sweetheart, who is an unmarried girl of the neighbourhood. He meets her in the veld at night or whenever and wherever he can. This is not considered by the Xhosa as immoral though it can end up in complications. Such love affairs are discussed elsewhere in this book in more detail.

Inheritance

The law of inheritance follows a specific pattern among the Xhosa and a man has only a limited say as to what must happen to his own possessions when he dies. Women and girls do not inherit. In fact, women own very little at any stage other than their own personal possessions and, of course, their 'cow of the home'.

The major beneficiary in an estate is always the man's eldest son, who is his heir. If the man had several wives, then the eldest son of his main wife benefits and his legacy is not only the majority of his father's cattle but also his dead father's responsibilities as head of the family. If the legator had no sons, then his brother or nearest male relative takes preference over his own wife and daughters. But then that man would have to ensure the family was cared for. The Xhosa are highly conscious of their responsibilities to their families and their homes and it would be exceptional to find a man who neglected these duties.

The inheritance law goes on in lengthy detail beyond this and allows for lesser portions to lesser sons and provides *inter alia* that where the main wife has no son then the son of a lesser wife may be elevated to the main house, but these details are of too technical a nature to be of interest here. It is, though, worth mentioning that where a father, before he dies, wishes certain cattle to go to a particular son, who by tradition would not ordinarily inherit, then he publicly donates them to the boy in front of witnesses. Then they become irrevocably his on his father's death and the rest of the herd is distributed in the normal course to the traditional heir or heirs.

Chapter 4   Life's First Rites

Phopho Lolombela beside a cool seaside pool. Like all Xhosa boys he loves water, and never misses an opportunity to swim. His name, Phopho, is his people's equivalent of paw-paw, the tropical fruit. Right: Girls in their "Sunday Best" share a calabash of sour milk. Their bodies are painted with red ochre. The posture of the girl on the ground is the typical resting position of girls and women who can remain comfortable sitting on their legs like this for long periods.

The Xhosa have large families and they regard fertility as a blessing.

Sterility is not common among them, but when it does occur in a young woman it causes a lot of concern. If the family think she has been bewitched, they get the advice of a witch-doctor who treats her with his magic medicine; where witchcraft is not suspected, her father has to fetch her back and shut her up in a small grass hut all alone for a month. During this time, in some strict families, she cannot be seen by anyone and may only go out in the dead of night when no-one else is about, but in others, today, the old custom of exclusion of contact is not so rigidly carried out. Her food is pushed in through a hole in the grass wall. When finally she comes out again, she will be able to have her baby.

This is a delayed form of what is known as the *Intonjane* ceremony which is usually performed in a girl's age of puberty and *before* her marriage. If it is not at that time performed, and she does not have a baby after marriage, the cause is attributed to the neglect and the ceremony is then carried out in the manner mentioned above. The *Intonjane* ceremony is not consistently carried out among the Xhosa today but in some of the older, tradition-conscious families, the ritual is stuck to religiously. It is accompanied by the slaughter of a beast and involves many other detailed procedures while the girl is in isolation.

Sex, among the Xhosa, is spoken of quite openly. It is something healthy and natural and is a normal aspect of everyday life. They live close to nature and take life as it comes. Sentimentality, insofar as it exists among the Xhosa,

is something much more rugged, down to earth and practical than it is among white people. Affection and family ties are strong and families and clans are bound tightly together, but men and women do not make an exhibition of their love, not to the outside world anyway.

Though I grew up in their midst and have lived in their proximity off and on for many years, I have never yet seen a man kiss his wife or a boy his girl friend. Even the holding of hands between young lovers in public is seen only very occasionally, and then usually in a momentary lighthearted gesture of teasing. A mother does sometimes kiss her nursing baby but even this outward sign of affection is not kept up to any obvious extent once the child is older. I remember when, as children, my brother and I went off to school a few miles away on horseback in the mornings, my mother would kiss us goodbye but, at the same time, the little Xhosa piccanin, Alven, who went with us to look after our horses while we were in school, would go without even an exchange of words with his mother. She was Noseven, our family cook.

Birth

Xhosa women bear their children without any fuss and ado. Right up to the end of their pregnancy they go about their home chores, carry wood and hoe their husband's mealie lands. Sometimes labour sets in unexpectedly while they are out in the lands and then it often happens that Xhosa women have their babies in the shade of a nearby tree and after the birth put the baby on their backs and go home.

It is more common, however, for a child to be born in the

family hut attended by a woman of the neighbourhood who acts as the midwife.

After the umbilical cord has been severed the midwife treats the child's wound with oil which she takes out of the stem of her pipe with a long dry stalk of grass. This particular pipe she uses is an important article and no one else may handle it or even touch it. The father is not allowed in the hut when the baby is born. To protect the child against evil spirits which might come into the hut, the mother hangs up special roots in the thatch above its sleeping place.

'Deny the Things You Know'

The first rite performed on a baby soon after it is born is that of 'passing it through the smoke'. For this, a special fire is made on the mud floor on the wife's side of the hut, which is on the right when entering the door, with light wood and green leaves of a particular tree. The fire is so made to give off a lot of smoke. When it is at its best, the mother cradles the child in her hands and in a rhythmic movement swings it back and forth through the smoke while she chants: 'Deny the things you know. Wush! Wush! Wush! See to it that your mother's ointment pot is never dry. Wush! Wush! Wush!' The Xhosa phraseology for this is: '*Uze ukhanyele into Uyaziyo, wush! wush! wush! Gqina ihlala likanyoko lingomi, wush! wush! wush!*'

This ceremony has tremendous significance in the child's later life because it means he must never betray his friends or give them away. Even though he knows they have done wrong, he is supposed to deny all knowledge and act as if he knew nothing. The Xhosa throughout their lives stick rigidly to this code given to them in their first hours of life, and it is an exasperating characteristic to anyone trying to question them because they simply answer, 'I do not know'. They are supposed to maintain this stand rigidly until they are given a clearance to divulge the true facts by someone older than or senior to themselves. If, on the other hand, a Xhosa ever does betray a fellow tribesman, then it is because he was 'not passed properly through the smoke when he was born'.

The second phrase in the rite, 'see to it that your mother's

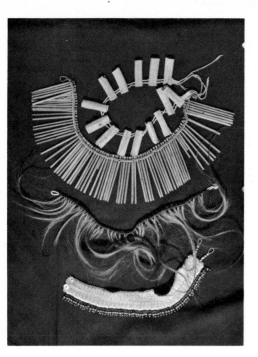

The necklaces worn by a young mother on the birth of her first child. The white blocks on the top piece signify that she is suckling a young baby.

Left: Dumane's second or "little" wife. Her headdress, the necklaces which she is wearing and her whitened face all show that she is nursing her first baby.

ointment pot is never dry', instructs the child not to neglect his mother, but always to give her what she needs. This instruction too is carried out religiously in after years and a mother can invariably rely on the support of her children.

Men Excluded

In most of the clans in the Ciskei the husband is not allowed to see his wife or the baby for the first four days after it is born and then his visit may only be a short one. After that he has to stay out for another three days before he can come back home to live. In the time that he is not permitted to be with his wife, he stays in the spare hut or storeroom, if he has one, or otherwise with friends in the neighbourhood. If, however, this causes hardship, then he can come home when the baby is four days old. In some clans there is a variation of this procedure: the husband is not prohibited from seeing his wife but acts as her liaison with those outside. In addition to the prohibition placed on her husband, the mother may not be seen by any other man at all until ten days after her baby is born. In the whole period of confinement she is cared for by her midwife. After a woman has had three children, her confinement period is reduced to eight days and she comes out on the morning of the ninth.

Mother and Child Emerge

At the end of the confinement period, but before she returns to normal life, the mother has to clean the hut and freshly smear the mud walls and floor with cow dung.

Then she washes her own and her baby's body and throws the water away so that it cannot be used by anyone else. After that she crushes up a type of white chalky stone into a powder, mixes it with water into a paste and paints their faces and visible parts of their bodies white. Alternatively, she uses a white chalk or clay which is dug out of the ground for the purpose. On the eleventh morning, she goes out of her hut with the baby secured on her back by a red blanket which covers the baby completely and is wrapped around both bodies. Anyone who wants to see the child has to pay the mother five cents for a peep and the money gathered in

this way is used to buy soap, sugar, tea, coffee and other goods for the home. This ceremony goes on for the first week and while it perhaps sounds a little mercenary, it can in a sense be compared with the white people's custom of bringing presents to the new-born child.

Protection the Magic Way

The young mother at this stage wears a necklace of small round lengths of root as thick as her small finger and nearly as long. Each piece is similarly painted white with clay or chalk. This necklace is a sign to all she meets that she is nursing a young baby. At the same time she wears another necklace made from the tail brush of her 'cow of the home'. This second necklace is to make her well and to keep away evil spirits. Her baby for this same purpose also wears a tiny necklace or arm band of hair but, in its case, the hair comes from the brush of the father's cow.

In some Xhosa circles these 'healing' necklaces are said to be worn only on instructions from a witch-doctor, but the people that I have questioned in the Ciskei say that their women wear them of their own accord whenever necessary for the sake of their health.

To bring the baby good fortune, the mother has a special root which she chews and spits over it. There is also a custom which is practised to stop the child getting thin and wasting away. It requires that the parents cut off the first joint of one of its little fingers. Fortunately this drastic custom is not observed rigidly in the tribe and it is today only in isolated families that it is continued, although I have often met older tribesmen with the end of one of their little fingers missing. Tribal law does not specifically lay down which of the two fingers has to be amputated but custom within a particular clan or family does.

For instance the man named Lolombela at Cove Rock near East London says that in his family they always cut off the first joint of the left little finger. He firmly believes that the operation is effective and stops the person from pining away.

57

Dumane's first or "big" wife and one of her children. She has been allowed to raise her headdress clear of her eyes because, having given him two grandchildren, she is now allowed to "look her father-in-law in the eyes".

Sacrifice of the White Goat

At some stage, in nearly all facets of Xhosa life, the sacrifice of a white goat is called for and a baby within the first days of its life has one slaughtered for it to make it grow up strong and healthy. Lolombela says that his people believe that everyone is born well and healthy 'because *Thixo* (God) does not make people that are sick'. But after they are born, evil influences and witches can make them ill and sickly, so a white goat is sacrificed for a baby, to immunise it against sickness and keep it healthy.

The animal is killed in the afternoon and in the process, before it dies, has to bleat to call the ancestral spirits.

If it does not, then panic sets in because it indicates that the spirits are displeased. In practice, it would be most unusual to find a goat that did not, in fact, cry terribly in these circumstances and this is no doubt one of the reasons why goats are popular for sacrifices. Cattle, on the other hand, when they are being offered, often give the parties making the sacrifice very grave worries by their stubbornness in the face of pain and their refusal to bellow or emit any sound. This aspect is discussed in detail elsewhere in this book.

The goat's flesh is not eaten on the night that the animal is killed but instead it is spread out on the branches of a mimosa tree near the home until the next morning. The family and friends then gather for a feast. But before the meat is roasted, the main tendon of one of the goat's hind legs is cut out to be used as a cord for the baby's necklace of cow tail hair. This is all part of the goat-sacrifice ritual and if the details are not followed the baby will be sickly afterwards. Sometimes, of course, the child does get sick even though these ceremonies have been performed and then the parents immediately call in a witch-doctor to ask his advice. He first finds some mysterious reason why the first sacrifice did not work; for instance, it could be because the ancestral spirits were not satisfied with that particular animal or that something was left out of the proceedings. Then the witch-doctor orders that another white goat must be killed for the child and its intestines ground up and rubbed over the baby's face and body. With the protection that this will offer, no more harm will come to the baby.

A Name for the Child

The Red Blanket child does not have a christening ceremony since his parents are pagans. He is named at any time within, perhaps, the first year and this is done quite unceremoniously and without any special function. The Xhosa have no vocabulary of common names and a child might be called anything that sounds appealing to the person naming it. The names of sons are always chosen by the grandfather on the father's side or, in his absence by the father, and of daughters by the grandmother on the mother's side or, in her absence by the mother. The two popular categories of names are, firstly, that which links the time of the birth of the child with some important event which took place about then, and the other is where the person naming the child simply likes the sound of any particular word and uses it as his child's name. The Red Blanket Xhosa do not know the date of their children's birthdays and the first system of naming accordingly serves a useful purpose because it tends to define the person's age in later life. For instance, if there are unseasonally heavy floods at the time a child is born he might be called 'The Big Rains', or if he is born when the mealie crops are, as a result, good, he could just as easily be named 'The Year of the Mealies'. Such phrases are usually expressed in a single word, which makes up the name.

The other system of choosing a name, that is one which has a pleasing sound, is well illustrated by the names chosen for Lolombela's two young sons. The one is called 'Chentula', which is the Xhosa for a particular type of garden hoe used by the Xhosa farm workers when weeding their employer's pineapple lands. The other is simply called 'Phopho', which is the Xhosa for paw-paw, the fruit.

I met another example of this in a Xhosa man who had once worked as a messenger for an oil company in East London before going back to his homestead to settle down with a wife. His first children were all boys and *he* named each of them after one of the oil company's products. Then a daughter arrived and his wife should have named that, (there were no grandparents available) but she had been so impressed by the names that her husband had given the boys that she asked him to choose one for her daughter too. He called it after another of the company's products!

Although the Red Blankets cannot read or write they can quote the names of their ancestors back through many generations. This is all the more surprising as the same surname is not perpetuated *in daily use* down the family tree. Their system is that the father's first name (or what would be the Christian name in a white man's equivalent) becomes his son's second name (or surname). As an example of how this works in practice, the family of Lolombela can again be taken. His father's first name was Mbangeli, so his name is Lolombela Mbangeli or Lolombela, son of Mbangeli. Lolombela's sons, however, now lose the 'surname' their father used and take, instead, his first name as their 'surname' and so they are Chentula Lolombela and Phopho Lolombela. *Their* sons, as brother's children, in turn will have different 'surnames' of Chentula and Phopho. The system does go further than this in that the Xhosa trace their lineage down the line of the past *heads* of their family to a common progenitor.

Complications do not end there either because the Xhosa have the further custom, once the eldest son becomes well known, of discontinuing calling the father by his own name. Instead, they call him 'the father of so-and-so'. The mother's name is substituted in the same way.

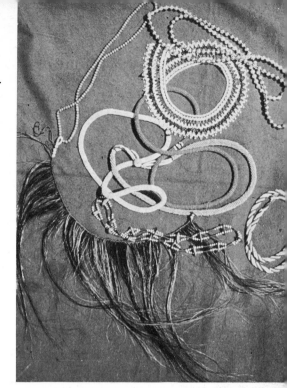

Above: These are the beads worn by Dumane's senior wife, who has two children and is not nursing either of them. She wears the magic necklace of the brush of her "cow of the home" when she feels it is necessary to keep herself healthy.

Below: A nursemaid and her charge. It is the accepted duty of every young girl to help any mother in the neighbourhood who needs assistance with her child. The duty of tending the fire and the pot also falls to her.

Helping Hands

It would often be an impossible task for a mother to handle her family of small children alone, in addition to her other duties of hoeing her husband's mealie lands, carrying wood from long distances, fetching water, keeping the mud floor and walls of her hut freshly smeared and cooking, if it was not for the help her elder daughters and the other women of the neighbourhood gave her.

Little girls help their mothers from the time they have barely learned to walk, and their first duty is to look after the smaller children of their own family but in addition, they also help other mothers of the kraal. Babies probably spend as much time on these volunteer nursemaids' backs as they do on their own mothers'. The women, too, help each other and assistance of this kind is hardly even regarded as a favour. It is taken for granted. It is part of the Xhosa way of life, and is automatic; the helper knows that just as he or she is good to someone today, someone else will in turn be as kind to them tomorrow. It is all part of their inbred open-house hospitality and mutual help system.

The baby's feeding time is often something of a social event for the women. They take this as an opportunity to sit around in a circle on the grass in front of one of their huts over a pipeful of tobacco. It is seldom that they all have pipes at the same time or, if they do, then at least some of them will be out of tobacco, so they are sociable and pass the available pipes around the circle for each to have a few puffs at a time. When the long stem of a pipe gets choked, one of the women picks a stalk of tough grass and pushes it through the stem to clean it. The grass comes out thick with a strong-smelling black pipe oil and many women suck this off the grass and eat it.

Time is of relatively little importance to the Xhosa in their kraals. They have no watches, and cannot tell the time anyway, so the sun and the dictates of nature guide them. If the sun is at a certain height, that might be the baby's feeding time and if the baby cries, it is hungry. When these things happen the mother sits down wherever she is and puts it to her breast. Nature has generously endowed Xhosa women and they are able to feed their babies up to an advanced age.

The man, in the Xhosa home, has little or nothing to do with bringing up the baby. He does not nurse it or carry it. Those are things for women to do. It is only when a child grows much older and has to be disciplined that he takes a hand. Then, as head of the family, in the case of boys in particular, he wields the rod and he wields it lustily. Xhosa children are brought up strictly. They must obey their parents, stick to etiquette in adult company and honour tribal customs and traditions.

The Way Around

One of the Red Blanket's strictest marriage laws is that imposed on a man and his wife when their baby is born. It is that, so long as a mother is suckling a child, another baby must not be conceived. They literally translate this to mean that in this time—which might easily be two years among the bantu—normal marital relations may not be resumed between the two of them. An interesting feature of this particular taboo, is that the Xhosa do not appear to attach the same importance to the possibility of the husband and wife each having secret affairs with an *outsider*. And it would perhaps not be incorrect to say that the Xhosa accept this as a way out even if they do not condone it. I questioned a Xhosa man on this subject and he said that extra-marital relations in circumstances of this kind do occur but 'it really is a dirty trick!'

He said that if a man found his wife and another man in a compromising situation of this kind the old Xhosa law would give him the right to kill both of them on the spot.

Should a woman at this time, in fact, have a child by someone else, then its father would have to pay her husband a penalty of at least seven head of cattle.

The husband, of course, has more official licence during this taboo period than his wife does because custom accepts that a man might, at any time, have a sweetheart in addition to his wife or wives. A corresponding privilege is never allowed to married women.

Chapter 5   Growing Up

Xhosa children live close to nature; they run around naked or near-naked most of the time and their parents do not pamper or spoil them. They live an open-air life in the wind, the weather and sunshine and they grow into tough and fine specimens of men and women.

'The Cattle of the Family'

The birth of a baby girl in a family creates a great deal of satisfaction because girls bring wealth to their father when, on their marriage, they earn *lobolo* for him from the husband who carries them off. This has given rise to the saying in the tribe that girls are 'the cattle of the family'. A man with many daughters regards himself as particularly well-favoured since he knows that the practice of polygamy enhances his opportunities for placing all his daughters on the marriage market at great advantage to himself.

Another feature of the marriage customs of the Xhosa which is in favour of the father of daughters is that, if he is worried about the possibility of any of them not being carried off in marriage, then he would be quite justified in approaching some man whom he thought suitable and suggesting to him that he took the girl as his wife. It would make no difference if the man concerned already had a wife or two. It is said that where a man is approached in this way he feels in honour bound to accept the girl and pay whatever *lobolo* is agreed upon with her father.

While daughters are welcomed for this significant reason, no equivalent mercenary value is attached to sons. It is, nevertheless, important for a man to have a son as an heir because daughters do not inherit nor are they regarded as perpetuators of the family line. Boys are also appreciated for the help they give their fathers.

It is interesting to note here that *boys* have no standing in Xhosa social status. They are regarded almost as not having arrived, they are spoken of as 'things' and the tribe actually have the saying about them that 'boys are dogs'.

As far as I have been able to interpret the working of the Xhosa mind on a boy's position in the structure of life, it is that while his body has arrived his spirit or soul has not. And so, in this state, he is just a 'thing'. He is incomplete. This position only changes and he 'becomes a person' after he has been through the circumcision rite in his late teens. Until this has happened he remains in a transitionary stage on earth. The period in life when this facet of a boy's make-up has perhaps the greatest significance is in his adolescent years. At this time young Xhosa are inclined to be wild and more irresponsible than usual, particularly if they have a wild streak in them. It is almost as if they trade on what is expected of them and that if everyone says that they are 'dogs' and 'things' then they can live up to it. On the other side of the scale their parents are possibly a little more tolerant of their mischief than they might be otherwise because, knowing that boys have no conscience, they have to make allowance for them. Not that boys can go *too* far, however, because if they have got strict parents they will not risk more than they think safe. In actual life one of the particular manifestations of 'being a dog' is that boys must boast that they will eat anything and be prepared to

support their claim. In practice, they actually do live up to the claim and will eat snakes, monkeys, polecats, dogs, jackals and anything of the kind that they are dared to eat but they do not, of course, have a regular diet of such things!

Childhood

The young life of Xhosa children is probably more carefree than that of white children of the same age. The little girls help their mothers from an early age and the boys get into trouble if they let their father's cattle stray, or do not have them home in time for milking, but on the whole they are carefree and happy and they are out in the sunshine from morning till night.

Boys in particular make the most of their childhood and in a day roam many miles through the countryside, swimming, hunting birds and small game, climbing trees and enjoying themselves wherever nature has something for them to do. Alternatively they will just as easily spend the whole day beside the river making clay oxen.

At an early age they become acquainted with the Xhosa names for every tree in their environment and get to know the kinds of wood which are strongest and best for hunting sticks and for fighting sticks. Then, too, they learn the names and habits of every wild animal, snake or insect and they can tell what bird has laid any egg they find even in the most secluded nest.

Birds, in one way or another, fill a lot of time in a boy's daily life, with probably most of that time taken in hunting them. For this sport boys carry half a dozen well-balanced throwing sticks and they comb the countryside in search of any particular birds they choose. They know where best to find the different species and how the bird is likely to take off when they do find it. Their idea is usually to bring it down in flight in an open area with a well-aimed throw.

Xhosa boys are expert at this game and I have often seen them even knock down quails in full flight. This is no easy task and I am not ashamed to say that I have tried it many

Opposite: Beadwork on boys of this age is not normal, so this little fellow could not resist the temptation of showing his off to his friends, even when he went for a swim.

Right: Mother and child.

Right: Like children everywhere, the Xhosa young learn by imitating their parents. This youngster is trying his hand at grinding maize into meal, but, finding the work a little heavy, decides to hand over to mother.

65

a time myself without ever so much as knocking a quail's feather out.

The idea in a bird hunt, apart from the element of sport, is to eat the birds killed. This adds a climax to the hunt.

It is remarkable how custom and necessity create habits in people in even the smallest things and, in this respect, I have in mind the particular way in which Xhosa boys carry the birds they kill. They hold them by their heads with the neck between their fingers and their bodies and feet dangling. I always thought this an ungainly and clumsy way of doing it, with the birds wings flopping around, until I analysed just why piccanins choose this way. The first reason is the obvious one that the boys have no pockets and the other is that by pushing the birds' necks between their fingers with the heads inside their hands they can carry half a dozen birds with ease in one hand and be quite comfortable. This leaves the other hand free to still carry a stick and to throw it if a target comes up. By comparison, a boy would not be able to carry more than one or two birds in his hand in a more conventional style.

After the hunt, boys always make for the riverside or some shady spot and roast their birds. In the case of doves and bigger birds, they pull the feathers off and clean them before roasting them, but the small birds they throw on the fire feathers and all and only after they are cooked do they clean them. This saves the bird burning away to nothing. The boys divide the meat with great care and they share and share alike. This is characteristic of Xhosa men, women and children; they share unselfishly.

But just as piccanins have this and many other fine characteristics in their dealings with each other, they can just as easily be cruel and lacking of any appreciation of the suffering they might cause an animal or some other creature. I remember in particular one day, when I was a child, some piccanins told me how, the day before, they had seen a hoopoe bird enter a hole in an antheap in search of food and how they had sneaked up on it and put a stone over the hole. That night they went back in the dark with some paraffin. They took the bird out, poured paraffin all over it, lit it and let it go. They shrieked with delight when they told me how a streak of fire flew into the dark and then just as suddenly, fluttered back to earth and died out.

Fireside Tales

It must be the custom for children everywhere to be told stories by their parents and, in this respect Xhosa are no exception. They too have their stories which cover folklore, mystery and magic and almost any event worth telling of, but mostly their stories are about things in nature; about frogs and hares and jackals, and about things mysterious like *Tikoloshe* the water sprite and *Ichanti* the water snake.

Folk tales and their origin are a study all of their own and no pretence is made here of giving the history of the one I relate below, except to say that it was told to me by a man named Mlomo (his name means 'mouth') in East London. He said it is a story which Xhosa parents like to tell to their children when they sit around the fire at night before they go to sleep.

Mlomo's story goes like this:

In the olden days men used to spend all their time drinking beer and the women had to plough the lands and hoe the mealies when they grew. When a certain man went to drink with his friends his wife would go to work in the lands. When she got there each day she put her baby under a tree in the shade and a dirty little animal, something like a person, used to come up from the river and look after it. The animal's name was Dlendle.

Then one day the mother had no food for her baby and it was crying when she put it down. When Dlendle came she said, 'Dlendle my baby is hungry, today I do not think you will be able to manage it, it will cry all the time'.

But Dlendle said, 'Mother, do not worry, I will do my best. I am sure I can manage the child'. So at last the woman gave up and left Dlendle and the child in the shade. While she was hoeing, Dlendle ate the child up but the woman did not see this. At sunset she came back and could find neither Dlendle nor her baby. She went down to the river and saw Dlendle sitting on the bank.

'Dlendle, where is my Baby? Bring it back,' she said. 'I have eaten your baby all up,' he answered.

The woman feared her husband greatly so when she went home she took a stone and put it on her back. When her husband came home in the evening, his wife was grinding mealies and the 'baby' was rolled up in blankets asleep.

'Woman,' said the husband who was sitting down smoking his long pipe 'Let me see the child.'

The woman would not take any notice of him but said 'Go yourself, and take the baby'. The man tried to pick up the child and said 'Ow! you have overfed this child today!' Then he saw that the baby had no mouth, no arms and no legs and that it was quite dead.

'Where is the child?' asked the man.

'It has been eaten by Dlendle,' answered the woman.

'What is *that*?' shouted the man.

'It is something like a man but not a man,' answered the woman.

'Where does it stay?' shouted the man.

'In the river,' she answered.

Then the man went out to discuss this with his friends and to get their help to trap Dlendle. He found out that Dlendle liked sour milk more than anything else that there is to eat. So the man and his friends took cans full of sour milk to the river and put them all around Dlendle's home. Then they got some ropes to catch the creature and went and hid where they could see what was going on but could not be seen themselves.

Dlendle came out and could see no one around. And he could not pass the milk because it was too tempting. So he drank and drank and drank. Then when he could hardly walk, the men rushed out and tied him up with their ropes and then killed him.

I was told another story by a man who had been to school and so was not a Red Blanket but his family, it seems, were. This story concerns his family and it is one which he insists is true.

He says that one day when he and his brothers were riding their donkeys home from school along a rough road, they saw another donkey racing ahead of them but with nobody on its back. It was kicking up clouds of dust. Something was clearly making it run like that. They tried to catch up with the animal but it seemed as if it was being spurred on. Then they saw something fall from its back, and when they got to that place they found an unusual kind of belt studded with pretty stones lying on the ground. They knew immediately that this was the belt of *Tikoloshe* the mischievous sprite. They were afraid to touch it at first but one of the boys said they should take it home to their father. And so they did. Their mother was terrified and said that the boys should take it straight back to where they had found it, but their father was excited and he said that he had never seen such a belt and was going to keep it. That night their father's eyes started getting sore and the one closed up and then the other and he could not see anything.

A game on the woodpile.

Right : A consultation on what is to be done after lunch.

Centre right : It is uncertain here whether the young lady has come to help or to nip out a morsel while no one is looking.

Far right : Lunch time.

68

He screamed with pain all that night and he never slept for an instant. He knew then that *Tikoloshe* was angry because they had taken his belt. No one could do anything in the dark and the father could hardly wait until it got light. Then he gave the boys the belt and said they should take it back to where they had found it.

While they were still away his eyes opened and suddenly there was no more pain and he knew then that at that instant *Tikoloshe* had found his belt.

Adolescence

I cannot think of the age of adolescence among young Xhosa without feeling that this is the period in their lives which they enjoy more than any other. The whole atmosphere of their lives at this stage is one of freedom and of happy abandon and one where they seem to have no cares in the world and will romp or dance and sing and play all day, or just as easily sit around for eight or more hours with not a thing to do except engage in light talk at the nearest trader's store.

Girls at this age are usually made to work in their father's mealie lands or tobacco patches during the week in addition to helping their mothers with the smaller children but they still find time to enjoy themselves, particularly at the week-ends. In these days-off they dress up in their best beads and their tiny skirts but wear little else—except that they may decorate their bodies with red ochre—and gather with the other girls of the same age group from miles around. Their meeting place is usually near where they know the boys of the neighbourhood will also be meeting. They travel on foot and often carry sticks in the same way that their boy friends do and, as if to give vent to their pent-up energy, they sometimes move at a slow jog-trot for miles on end.

Periodically they stop to join in light games of fighting with their sticks or just to dance and sing. Their dance is of the same type as that of the boys with emphasis on body movements, the stamping of the feet and on arm movements. They dance individually or in small groups or in large troupes.

Left: A typical resting position of young Xhosa boys and men. It is traditional and allows them to leap into action at the least sign of danger.

Above: Two young Xhosa have a parley beside the colourful old chief Dlambe's "throne" at Macleantown.

Above right: Xhosa boys marshalling for a knobkerrie fight while the girls clap and sing as they watch. This is a small part of the group involved in the incident described in the book which might have ended in disaster "because of photography".

The adolescent boys at the same time gather at their meeting ground from all over the neighbourhood and make a tremendous noise with cheap whistles, concertinas and guitars as they trot along to their destination. For such occasions, as opposed to their purely social Sunday-best outfits, the boys dress in the minimum of clothing, particularly if they plan to have fighting matches. The most they are likely to wear on an outing like this is a legging or two of Angora goat skin or of dry cocoons filled with pebbles to make them rattle, a high peak cap, a small red blanket-wrap around the waist or just a sheath made from skunk or monkey skin with tassels down to the ground and a few beads. The beads might, however, be left at home altogether if fighting is to be indulged in. Outfits like this are worn in the more secluded areas but if the boys have to pass along public roads then they will be reasonably well-covered.

In an afternoon's fun the boys mix fighting with dancing.

They parade around in large groups and their dance consists of wild jumping and stamping movements to the accompaniment of singing and musical instruments. Their girl friends either watch the boys or join in the fun themselves. In their stick fights the boys start off in playful mood fighting against each other in pairs or on chosen sides but frequently when someone starts hitting harder than he should, tempers flare and quite often skulls are cracked and boys sometimes even get killed. The unfortunate part about incidents like this is that, once they happen, the boys then pick sides the following week and go back to get revenge. After this, trouble can really build up and what started as a game can end in ugly scenes.

Another form of dancing that young Xhosa indulge in is that of a controlled system of vibrating or rippling their chest and abdomen muscles. It is a form of dancing which it seems is practised almost exclusively by the Xhosa.

71

A spontaneous picture of Xhosa boys at their favourite pastimes of dancing and stick fighting. On these occasions the boys dance in big groups while scores of scantily clad girls form the audience and clap out an accompaniment. At intervals the girls form up in their own teams and dance opposite the boys.

At the end of an afternoon's session of fun the boys and girls gather together at one or other kraal and go on with their dance, or *Xhentsa* as they call it, and their melodious harmonising can be heard for long distances.

Then, as the night wears on, it is accepted practice for boys and girls to pair off together and make their ways into quiet corners in the dark. This is a recognised routine and they spend the night together out in the bushes. Xhosa custom, however, instils into the young ones a strict code of discipline which must be observed on these occasions because it would be a terrible disgrace if a girl were to fall into trouble by a boy who had not yet been through the initiation ceremony and become a man. This kind of love-making is known as *Ukumetsha*.

An example of how the Xhosa regard boys (uncircumcised males) in so far as any serious association with a girl is concerned came to my notice in the case of a family at Kei Road. The particular incident occurred when, after a certain young girl had been carried off in marriage, in orthodox fashion, her younger sister was so impressed with the idea of marriage that she ran away with a *boy* of about nineteen years of age. Such a thing is almost unheard of in Xhosa circles but it was said that the boy was a known rascal. The incident stunned the girl's parents and her father immediately set out on horseback to find her and bring her back.

The grapevine is strong in Xhosa circles and no one can go on any road without being seen by someone who knows them and so the pursuer was able to track the couple down to a kraal forty miles away. But by the time he got there the two had had warning of his coming and fled but with so little time to spare that she left all her clothes behind except the skirt she was in. In his fury her father then publicly disowned her and took her clothing back home with him.

It would be interesting to know what the outcome of this story would have been in the normal course of events and whether the two would have been in a position to settle down in the tribe as man and wife and have a family and, if they were, to what extent they would have been accepted in social circles. But fate stepped in and subsequent unconfirmed reports have it that the boy was caught by the law on some criminal charge at that time and was taken into custody for a long period. The family, when last I heard, did not know what had happened to the girl, nor were they interested.

A Girl's Married Sweetheart

When a Xhosa boy and girl begin to like each other sufficiently to be sweethearts then the girl has to discuss their case with her mother and get her formal permission before their association can continue. If the mother likes the boy she gives her consent and the two are accepted as sweethearts. There is no suggestion, however, of ultimate marriage in such a formally blessed relationship. It is purely a 'boy and girl affair' and one which is expected to play no part when later the boy becomes a young man and has to find a wife.

In the same way that such a girl might have a boy as her particular friend, so another might have a *married man*. Unlike the marriage routine, however, where a man may choose a complete *stranger* to be his wife, this lover arrangement is more likely to be between a man and a girl who already know each other and perhaps have become more than normally friendly. The man, in this case, approaches the girl when she is alone and asks her if she will be his sweetheart (the Xhosa often use the actual English word 'sweetheart'). If she does not like him sufficiently she will say 'no' outright but if she does like him then she still dare not agree of her own accord but, again, has to discuss the matter with her mother and ask for her permission.

Occasions of this kind are among the few when a married woman has any final say in family affairs. If a mother were to refuse her consent to a girl associating in the proposed manner with a man, then that would be final and the girl would obey, despite her own feelings, because tribal custom and family rules have to be adhered to.

If, on the other hand, the mother liked the man it would be in order for her to agree to her daughter establishing a

At the approach of the camera a group of girls pause for a moment in their song—their hands still in the clapping position. Singing and dancing among the Xhosa is always accompanied by handclapping.

Below: A Xhosa boy relaxing with two friends. The kilt-like skirt that he is wearing has a special significance as it was given to him by his sweetheart. In Xhosa tradition the wearing of such an article is a boast to his friends that he has made the conquest of a heart.

relationship with him but the mother would not tell her husband, the girl's father, of the arrangement or that she had given her consent to it.

These arrangements are purely extra-marital and, again, there is no suggestion in them of any ultimate marriage. With the mother's consent obtained, the couple meet in secret usually at night in the veld or whenever and wherever opportunity affords, but the man must never be seen at the girl's family hut nor may he openly identify himself with her in any way.

An authority on Xhosa customs to whom I referred this subject says that there is even an accepted procedure which is followed when they meet in that the man is expected to place his blanket-wrap on the ground and sit on it and she in turn drops hers on top of his and joins him. This apparently is their formal indication of their mutual affections and of an offer made and accepted. I enquired how a married man was able to be absent from his wife and home, perhaps for a whole night and I was reminded that a Xhosa man is master in his own home and if he chooses to be away from it then that is his affair and if his wife takes him to task on it she might end up with a sore ear! The question of the girl explaining her movements would not be quite so straightforward but, with her mother's co-operation, she could easily be away 'visiting friends' when an occasion demanded.

It happens, of course, that a girl and her lover might have a child and then complications set in. The girl's father taxes his wife on why he was not told of their daughter's affair and goes to the wife of the man he suspects and demands to know if it is her husband who has been associating with his daughter. The outcome of the situation is that when he establishes who the child's father is he demands payment in cattle from him as compensation. The number called for would probably be at least seven head. The girl's parents then normally bring up the child as if it was their own.

If the girl should subsequently have another child by the same or another man, the father would again have to pay a penalty or compensation to her father but this time it would not be so many cattle. In circumstances of this kind

where a girl has had a child or children then, in her subsequent marriage, her *lobolo* would not be quite as high as it would ordinarily have been, but the Xhosa do not attach any stigma to such a girl and men I have questioned express indifference to the fact. They just shrug their shoulders and say, 'what does it matter?'

In regard to an unmarried mother's actual eligibility for marriage, one man classified her as being in the same category as a widow with children though, he said, when the *girl* gets married there is a pretence at a 'carrying off' marriage ceremony though no prior arrangements are made with her father for her hand. Instead, the girl and the man just agree to marry and the man thereafter goes to her hut and carries her off. She pretends to resist and screams and shouts, 'but,' my informant said, 'if she overdoes her protests he beats her with his stick and chases her back to his home'. Only after he has taken her away does he go and discuss the *lobolo* payment with the father. On enquiring how many cattle would be paid for a girl like this, I was told 'not *many* less because, after all, if the girl has got daughters then they will bring her husband cattle or, if she has got sons, they will work for him!'

In the instance of a widow marrying the second time, the bridegroom merely arranges with her that she should come and live with him as his wife and that he will take her children as well. In this case he would still pay *lobolo*, but not so many cattle, and he would pay it to her eldest son or to her late husband's heir whoever he was.

Their Way of Thinking

It is purely coincidental that this subheading dealing with the mentality and ways of thinking of the Xhosa is included in a chapter dealing with boys and girls, but it just happened that the three episodes related below most vitally concerned boys. The reactions of the people, however, are the same in

The boys take their national sport seriously and many is the boy who ends up with a cracked skull. Tempers often flare in battle and what started as a game often ends up in an ugly mood and sometimes even faction fights between clans.

all their ages whether it is of a child, adolescent or adult. All of the incidents related occurred while I was taking photographs for this book. In fact they occurred because I was taking them.

On the first occasion, I was working on a collection of witch-doctor pictures at the kraal on a farm where much of my material has been gathered, and where all the Xhosa know me well and co-operate happily whenever I take photographs there.

On this particular day I had my cameras set up and was not paying any special attention to the fact that a big crowd had gathered around, as always happens when anything is going on in Xhosa circles, or to the fact that many young adolescents were having mock battles nearby with their sticks. Then suddenly a woman screamed angrily:

'Just look at this! This is because of photography! If there were no cameras this would never have happened. Just look, this boy is going to die!'

I did look and found myself facing half a dozen women, all equally arrogant. Behind them stood a youth with blood streaming down the side of his face and next to him a group of his friends covered with sweat and flecks of blood. Their sticks were frozen in the positions in which they had stopped fighting. I realised immediately what the consequences could be. If the camera was to blame, their vengeance might be taken out on the camera and possibly not only on that but also on its operator. Me!

But this was the day that I thanked my stars that I speak Xhosa and understand something of the Xhosa mind. I looked at the woman and past her at the boys and, with a touch of scorn, said: 'Ow! but I thought these were *big* boys, I thought they had grown up and learned to fight like men do, yet I see they lose their tempers! When big boys fight they are supposed to control themselves like big people do because, otherwise, if they get cross, they get hurt. Ow! you

A trio in their "Sunday-Best".

must never forget, young men, you are Xhosa and Xhosa know how to fight with sticks.'

I bent over my camera and went on supposedly viewing. Past the side of the camera, I noticed the blank look on many faces as the remarks sunk in and the crowd slowly tried to sort out what it was all about. Then I saw one woman spit vehemently towards the boys as she said viciously 'Hamba!' (go!) and stop being silly. You heard what Boss Aubrey said.' The spell was broken.

The second episode was really frightening though I must admit that in it I did take a calculated risk.

It was a Sunday afternoon and I was in the Kei Mouth area where the Xhosa are still more 'raw' than in most parts where the Red Blankets are still found. With this in mind, I was out on the public road with my son, Wayne, of thirteen, in the car and armed with my cameras.

On Sundays, when they have a holiday from their farmer employers, the men and women, boys and girls all dress up in their very best regalia and walk along the open roads in the area on their way to visit other kraals and, in the case of adults, to attend beer-drinks. I was hoping for some good photographs and I might have got them had circumstances been a little more favourable but as it happened it did not work out that way.

We were travelling slowly as we came over a rise in the road when unexpectedly we found the way ahead blocked for hundreds of yards with a mass of big Xhosa boys in their late teens. They were stripped for fighting and wearing little more than loin cloths. The boys were moving three abreast across the width of the gravel road with their sticks in the ready position. They were dead silent. Their silence alone was bewildering in its unusualness. I stopped the car not knowing what was going to happen next and then, still without a word, the ranks parted up the middle, two wide

The Xhosa live close to nature and water plays an important part in the tribe's life. These girls have painted their bodies with red ochre "to be attractive to the boys".

on one side of the road and one on the other, for me to pass. I half reached for a camera but saw the questioning look in Wayne's eyes, which said, 'Dad, are you doing the right thing?'

I could sense these youths were in no mood to be tampered with and I drove on slowly through the silent mass realising I was missing the chance of a lifetime, but I knew I was doing the only sensible thing just then. Two factors were important in this decision, the one was the ugly mood of the boys who were on their way to a fighting ground and the other was that, whenever Xhosa are photographed, they insist on being tipped and that would have been impossible in this crowd because each one would have expected something. Once we had got to the end of the rows Wayne said courageously, 'Dad, you know you have come seven hundred miles for this. If you want to, stop, I don't mind.' We looked around to see if the doors were locked. He was right—we had travelled all the way from Pretoria for just such a scene and were now seeing it slip by. But even so, my knowledge of the mentality and reactions of boys like this had taught me discretion and so we went on.

Once completely through the crowd I stopped the car and took a deep breath. We debated: 'What now?' Then I noticed the petrol gauge was fluttering on 'E'. Wayne said, 'What would have happened if we had run out of petrol in there? The nearest petrol station was fifteen miles away so that was our immediate destination. After that we had to return the way we came and we found the boys had moved on some distance from where we passed them. The picture now was somewhat different. They had been in a bloody fight but they were still well disciplined and opened out for us to pass. As we drove through the horde many were within a foot or two of the car and we gaped at some of the ugly gashes and blood spattered heads and bodies shiny with perspiration, but I knew better than to even show a camera now. When we got towards the end of the line, however, I agreed with Wayne that we should keep the doors locked and the windows closed and I would stop the car for just a moment with the engine running and lean out

of the driver's door and take a picture or two then drive on again quickly. I did so and in seconds there were shouts of 'He is taking photographs! He must pay us!' There was a surge towards the car but fortunately I had been expecting this and had a handful of small change ready. I poured it into the first out-thrust hands and let the clutch out. It lulled the crowd instantly and the nearest ones hurried up to see what I had given them but I lost no time in waiting for the results. By the time I heard them exclaiming that they wanted more '*bhasela*', (tip) I was under way but that is where I had to be doubly careful because had I bumped anyone, we would have been mobbed. After all this the pictures were not successful!

The third incident was of a different nature and I have always thought it rather amusing, particularly since the male character in it showed far more ingenuity than one normally finds among the raw Xhosa. I suspect he must have worked on the mines in Johannesburg at some stage and learned something of the white man's ways of business.

Again this time, I was in the Kei Mouth area when I came on a group of about twenty dancing girls rigged out in their best beads and outfits, so I stopped to ask if I could photograph them. They agreed, but wanted to know how much I would give them for one photograph. I said fifteen cents each. They exclaimed loudly, but more as a token than as a genuine resistance, and said that that was not enough but if I put down seventy-five cents (a total amount) on the stone beside the road (so that they could see that I was not going to drive on without paying them) all twenty of them would pose for me! If I had attempted to correct them they would have thought I was out to cheat them so I agreed and put the money down. As I was setting up my tripod there was an equally amusing sequel to this when a young Xhosa beau came along and called me aside. He asked what I had agreed to pay the girls. I told him and he said: 'No! that is not enough!' He said I must pay R1 (100 cents) but not to them because he was their manager and he would collect it and distribute it . . . seventy-five cents to them and twenty-five to himself for his services!

Chapter 6   Initiation to Manhood

The Abakwetha *hut is usually in the loneliest spot available. The initiates may not in any circumstances see or be seen by a married woman during their period of isolation. The little boy on the right is the lackey of the "school".*

In a previous chapter I mentioned that a boy among the Xhosa is a 'thing' and not a person and that he only emerges from this state, to become a man, after he has been through the tribe's circumcision rite. This rite is known as the *Ukwalusa* (circumcision) or the *Abakwetha** ritual and it is the most important event in any male's life. His age, in later life, is quoted in relation to the time when he was an *umkwetha* in the initiation school and so are any important happenings which take place after he has been through this ceremony.†

The full ritual is spread over a period of about three months, and the two most important individual aspects of it are the 'going in', (which involves the actual circumcision) and the 'coming out', which takes place at the end of a period of isolation to which the initiates are subjected after the surgical operation.

The Sobering Effect

The event usually takes place in the boy's late teens but sometimes, when they are particularly wild and cannot be controlled by their parents, boys are put in earlier to sober them up and to instil responsibility into them. The interesting part about the rite is that it indisputably does have this effect. The reason is not because of any punishment or discipline that is exercised over the initiate in the school itself but purely, it seems, because of the psychological power the rite has. I have known cases of widows whose sons, without a father's restraint, were quite out of control and

---

* The 'h' in this word is silent. *Abakwetha* are the initiates (plural) and *Umkwetha* is singular.
† The Red Blanket Xhosa are illiterate and so do not have written records.

---

spent their time thieving and getting up to all the mischief imaginable, who in the end were physically caught by the men of a kraal and taken struggling and shouting to the surgeon with his sharpened assegai. They were in each case completely reformed as a result of the ceremony. It is perhaps interesting to relate here that, in the case of one of the boys concerned, his mother ran after him as he was dragged away and shouted 'Hamba! Hamba! Hamba!' ('Go! Go! Go!'). This command was not to the boy himself but to the evil and wicked influences in him that they should get out of his body.

Going In

The routine in an initiation ceremony may differ in minor detail in the different clans of a tribe and in different areas but such differences are only in procedure and not in basic principles. The routine described below is that which is common on the Ciskei farms.

The time of the year when a school starts usually coincides with the ripening of the annual maize crop, which is about March or later, and the number in the school depends on the number of eligible boys in the right age group in the immediate locality at the time. On the Ciskei farms this is usually about three or four.

Mostly, a going-in ceremony takes place at a week-end when working people are free to attend. First, on the Friday afternoon, each candidate has his head shaved by a man of his kraal, and is given a necklace made of the tailbrush of his father's 'Cow of the Home'. This necklace is a circlet with the hair knotted at four equal intervals around its circumference and is a supplication to the boy's ancestors to give him wisdom and strength. He is also given a new pure white cotton baize blanket or a sheepskin kaross to use while he is in isolation, and a new knobkerrie and a sharp assegai. The tradition behind the assegai is that if, while he is in the school, anyone brings him stolen food to eat, he will be able to kill him.

On this same Friday afternoon a goat (of any colour) is killed for each boy at his own home, and each has to sit in the cattle byre, where most offerings are made, and eat the animal's whole right foreleg after it has been lightly boiled. They are not allowed to have any salt with it and may not eat any of the fat. Their families and their guests then eat the rest of the goat.

After their respective meat-eating episodes, the boys all make their way to the kraal of the particular father who initiated their school and who is known as the *sosuthu* (or as expressed in the Xhosa language, the *usosuthu*)*. He is always supposed to be a very respected person and is regarded as the 'senior' father.

As night falls on the Friday night, the boys and girls of the neighbourhood arrive for an all-night dancing session at which the boys all dance naked or near-naked. After this evening, the initiates are not allowed again to wear anything that they wore as boys, and all their clothes are given away to their younger friends.

At dawn on the Saturday morning, the man who is to be in charge of the initiates' school during its period of existence, and who is known as the *khankatha**, arrives and calls the initiates together. At this stage the girls who danced during the night with them, run down to the river to wash. The implication of this is that they wash away the things of their past and leave behind their childishness to enter a new age with the initiates. At the river they discard the beads and baubles that they wore during the night, and from this time on they wear longer skirts and are known as 'young men's girls' and not 'boys' girls'.

* The role of *sosuthu* it seems is not common to initiate schools in all areas. In some, the *khankatha*, apparently, takes his place, but in ceremonies which I have personally witnessed in the East London area, the *sosuthu* has played an important role.

After the initiates have been called together the *khankatha* and several other men all carrying knobkerries surround them, in case they decide to run away, and then take them down to the river to wash away *their* past. At the water the boys bend down and throw water once over the front of their bodies and once over the back. Then they are taken to a place where they await the surgeon who is to perform the operation on them. The 'surgeon' has no medical qualifications and is merely a man who has been taught by one of his fellows to perform the circumcision operation. This spot is invariably near the little 'beehive' grass hut in which they live during their isolation. Naked and shivering with cold and fright, they sit down and wait in the company of men of the neighbourhood. No women are allowed near this scene.

The Surgeon *(Incibi)* Arrives

At sunrise, or thereabouts, the surgeon arrives and can be heard coming in the distance because, as he passes the family huts, the women set up an incessant 'Wululululu' wailing which is quite terrifying in its effect. In the process of welcoming the doctor, those whom he passes have to be careful because he is a temperamental fellow who trades on reputation and flails his arms and his assegai around, not minding if he hurts anyone in the process if they get too close to him.

As the doctor comes in sight of the initiates, he starts ranting and abusing and screaming at them and viciously shouts 'Where are these DOGS, where are these THINGS that I have come to make men?' At the same time he loudly exhorts the badness and the evil to be gone out of them so that they may be men whose childish things are past. The surgeon then suddenly swings his assegai out dramatically in front of the boys and prepares for the operation.

This is done with a deft stroke of the sharpened blade and the boy must not cry out or even flinch in pain. As he operates the doctor says, 'You are a man!' and makes a low growling noise in his throat as he throws the excised portion on the ground in front of the initiate who has to repeat 'I am a man!' as he picks up the portion and holds it in his clenched hand while the doctor passes on to the next in line. After this, the initiates have to go in different directions and bury the portions in an antheap where the ants will eat them up so that a sorcerer cannot find them and make medicine from them. If the portions *were* used for such a purpose then the initiates' wounds would never heal. An alternative place of burial is in the floor of the new hut where, in the process of burying them the initiates sit with their backs towards the centre of the hut, and facing away from each other, so that no one of them can see what the other is doing.

The wound is bound by the *khankatha* with special leaves which are supposed to have healing properties and mud is then packed over them or, alternatively, pulped rushes are tied around the leaves.

The surgeon then smears a mixture of antheap and water on the face and chest of the initiates and makes them drink a mouthful of the mixture. This makes their hearts hard like antheap, so that they will not be cowards in their future lives as men. It also prevents them from getting dizzy.* The initiates are next painted white with chalk or clay from head to foot and then they wrap themselves up in their new blankets so that they will not catch cold. While this is happening their *khankatha* lectures them on how to behave as *abakwetha*, telling them that they must not steal or do anything that an honourable Xhosa man would not do. The surgeon's duty, after this, is finished and after being paid *50 cents* by the father of each initiate, he goes on his way.

The Khankatha

After this, the initiates are marched off to their new grass hut and are left to themselves and to their misery. To help them and to serve as their lackey, they are given a young piccanin who has to stay with them throughout their period in the school. This piccanin is known as their 'little *khankatha*'

---

* The Xhosa know no medical terms for describing their ailments but have a fixed set of descriptions which broadly cover the area of the body. For instance in the case of almost any abdominal pains they say they 'have a stomach'. For a headache they 'have a head', for any chest trouble they 'have a chest', and a particularly popular form of illness is 'to be dizzy'.

and he is responsible for fetching and carrying their food and all their needs from the kraals of the respective parents, after it has first been brought to the *sosuthu's* hut. Throughout the period of isolation, which in the Ciskei is about three months, he paints himself white like the *abakwetha* and he goes wherever they go. Traditionally, the adult *khankatha* is responsible for the well-being of the initiates and, according to old custom, he should live with them; in practice, in the small schools, this system is not kept up today because a Xhosa man is a bread-winner and his time usually cannot be spared. The adult *khankatha* does, however, remain in overall charge of the group throughout the initiation period and sees that they behave themselves, that they are looked after and that the various sequences of the *Abakwetha* rite are followed.

In particular, he has to teach them a special vocabulary of words which they have to use while in the school. The use of these words is known as *hlonipha*.

Hlonipha

Hlonipha in this case is the use of substitute words in the place of other everyday words which may not be used at any time while the initiates are in the school. The basic idea of the custom is to show respect and subservience and it is the same custom which is used by a bride to show respect to her father-in-law. In the case of the *abakwetha*, it is not so clearly defined, however, as to who in particular is being shown respect, although they do have to show special regard for *married* women. It seems that one of the main reasons for them carrying out the practice is that they have to admit their own 'littleness'. They are not yet real men and in this position must show their own unimportance.

The First Seven Days

For the first seven days after their operation, the initiates hardly leave the hut and so stay shut up in the dark. This is partly through discomfort and lack of any interest in moving around and partly because it is the custom. All their food is supplied by their own parents but, before it comes to the

initiates' hut, it has to be taken to the home of the senior father (the *sosuthu*) and cooked by the women there. The little piccanin lackey then fetches it from that hut. In this first week, the diet is austere and consists only of dry maize grain which is very lightly boiled and eaten hard, while the only liquid that may be drunk is water mixed with antheap or fine ash into mud.

On the eighth day, which is usually a Sunday, the joint fathers give the adult *khankatha* a goat to slaughter at the *abakwetha* hut. This is to 'return the initiates to normal eating again'. All the menfolk of the neighbourhood gather at the hut for this ceremony and the initiates all have to strip for the men to examine their wounds and to discuss them.

When the examination is over the initiates are given the right foreleg of the goat to roast on the coals of a fire made of sneezewood; the foreleg has been fouled with the green leaves of the same tree to give the meat a bitter taste. The meat is further spoiled by being put in the ashes of the fire.

When the meat is ready, the 'big' *khankatha* puts pieces of it in the thorny branches of a mimosa tree and makes the initiates take them from there with their mouths. While they are trying to do so, he turns the branches so that the thorns stick them in the face. This is to strengthen them to resist

Above left: Abakwetha. These young men are Abakwetha or "initiates to manhood". The full right of attaining manhood is spread over a period of three months or more and involves several important ceremonies. During this time the initiates are isolated from the normal activities of their home kraals.

Above right: Inside an Abakwetha hut. The suspended bed is the product of the originality of one of the "school". The fire on the floor is a feature of all Xhosa huts.

Left: Having completed their period of isolation, the Abakwetha prepare to go down to the river to wash away their past. Their lackey, who goes through much of the ritual with them, is in the foreground.

Right: Their lackey goes through the same washing ritual as the Abakwetha themselves do.

evil influences in their life ahead. The carcase of the goat is then cut down the middle and the side from which the foreleg was taken – that is the right side – is given to the initiates to keep and eat in the ordinary way. The left side is eaten, on the spot, by the men present while the liver, the head, the trotters, the entrails and the skin are given to the *khankatha* to take home with him.

Breaking the Ice

On the third Sunday, that is on the sixteenth day, the girls of the neighbourhood are brought to meet the *abakwetha*. For the occasion, the 'big' *khankatha* makes the initiates freshen up their white paint and he gathers all the local girls in their best beads and skirts and takes them along to the hut. This is a particularly formal occasion, however, and the initiates are made to sit on the ground in a row with the girls sitting down facing them, also in a row.

This ceremony is to break the ice and to let down the temporary barriers which were set up to prevent the initiates meeting any females in their first two weeks. After this meeting, the initiates are again allowed to associate with girls and join them in the prescribed love-making, known as *ukumetsha*, at night but they still may not see or be seen by married women. If one comes into sight, they have hurriedly to cover their faces.

If, during their isolation, any of the initiates want anything from home, they can only go there at night but have to be careful that their *mothers* do not see them (their sisters and unmarried girls do not matter). They can not go into the hut but, instead, have to sit in the cattle pen and hit their two sticks together to draw attention. Whoever hears them, sends a piccanin to find out what they want.

The adult *khankatha*, as their guardian, often visits the initiates at their hut and as he approaches he has to emit a shrill whistle to announce his coming and they in turn have to whistle back to acknowledge that they have heard him. If they do not do this, the *khankatha* hits their hands with a switch as punishment.

87

Abakwetha Dances

A feature of the big initiation schools of the Transkei is the spectacular dances in which the *abakwetha* dress up in grass skirts and elaborate headdress, but in the small schools on the farms in the Ciskei this does not take place. These dances are today regarded as good healthy entertainment but I feel this chapter would be lacking if I failed to quote something of their past history and of the light in which the dances were regarded a hundred years ago.

The following description of the dance, which is referred to as the *Ukutshila**, was given in notes written by a Mr. Warner – who was a Government representative known as the 'Tamboekie Agent'. They were written at the request of Colonel Maclean c.b., Chief Commissioner in British Kaffaria who resided at Fort Murray, near King Williams Town.† The notes are dated the 1st December, 1856 and read: 'Another heathenish custom connected with this rite†† is the "*Ukushila*" and which consists in attiring themselves with the leaves of the wild date in the most fantastic manner; and thus attired, they visit each of the kraals to which they belong, in rotation, for the purpose of dancing. These "*Ukushila*" dances are the most lewd and licentious which can be imagined. The women act a prominent part in them, and endeavour to excite the passions of the novices (initiates) by performing all sorts of obscene gesticulations.'

In further deriding the *abakwetha* ritual, Mr Warner had the following to say in telling of the initiates themselves: '. . . they are, as it were, let loose on society, and exempted from nearly all restraints of law, so that even should they steal and slaughter their neighbour's cattle, they would not be punished; and they have the special privilege of seizing by force – if force be necessary – every unmarried woman they choose for the purpose of gratifying their passions.'

Mr. Warner ends his discussions with: '. . . every endeavour ought to be made to do away with, at least, all the objectionable and heathenish parts of the rite.'

* This is the modern spelling.
† From 'A compendium of Kaffir Laws and Customs' compiled by direction of Colonel Maclean c.b.
†† The circumcision ceremony.

It is pleasing to report here that the *abakwetha* rite, today, does not include the objectionable characteristics he mentions. In fact, the doctrine of the new rite is that the initiates should behave themselves and specifically that they should not allow anything stolen to come into their hut.

Time on Their Hands

During the period of isolation in the *abakwetha* school, the initiates have a leisurely, lazy time with nothing specific to occupy their days. They sometimes work in the mealie lands, provided there are no married women about, but it is much more common for them to roam the veld with their little *khankatha* and a dog or two, hunting birds and hares. Then at other times they meet the unmarried girls of the kraal and spend hours in light chatter at the *abakwetha* hut.

Coming Out

After about three months, the time arrives for the coming out ceremony. This is an important event in their young lives and is performed with a great deal of pomp combined with intense solemnity. It is a serious occasion and the initiates are made to realise it to the full. It is a rite which instils deeply the significance of being a *man* and of assuming the responsibilities which go with it, because the man, in the Xhosa world, is everything. All life, and life-hereafter, revolves around him.

The actual coming out ceremony is usually on a Saturday but the proceedings start on the Friday evening when the initiates are brought, heavily blanketed so that no married women will see their faces, from their own little hut to the home of the senior father (that is the *sosuthu*), where they have to spend the night in the cattle byre. Here the 'big' *khankatha* cuts their hair short. Sometimes, however, their hair is shaved a few days before this so that by the time the day of coming out arrives, it has grown sufficiently to cover their bald scalps.

As evening approaches, guests start arriving to attend the next day's ceremony and they bring with them their own beer because it would be difficult and expensive for the *sosuthu* to make beer for everyone, though he does supply boiled mealies and, perhaps, meat. He also provides coffee and tea.

On the Friday night the initiates make themselves a fire in the byre (the cattle do not sleep in it that night), and throughout the night they noisily play a popular Xhosa game with pebbles in which each one has to guess in which hand the others are holding their pebbles. The menfolk play the same game on their own outside and the women chatter and talk in the huts. They all drink beer, but no one is particularly interested if the food runs out. The girls and boys for their part dance and sing outside. No one sleeps at all.

At sunrise the *khankatha* 'wakes' the initiates and tells them to be ready to go back to their hut for the next stage of the ceremony. This is the washing away of the past; the anointing with butter and the burning of the hut.

I was fortunate in being able to attend such a ceremony and was most impressed with the ritual and its manifestation of centuries of tradition, though I could not help wondering how it all originated and where. There seemed to be such a strong link here with a distant past. Yet the Xhosa themselves know nothing of its origin. They do not even know *why* they follow the routine. They just know that it is a Xhosa ritual and that, if they do not follow it in detail, everything will go wrong with the *abakwetha* because they would not have been made men in the right way. The ceremony started at sunrise and I had as my guide Lolombela Mbangele.

At the farm on which the ceremony was taking place, we stopped at the farmer's homestead and Lolombela asked me to wait while he went to discuss matters with the *sosuthu* and the *khankatha* and get their permission for me to watch the proceedings. He was away all of half an hour and I was getting anxious to know why, when he sent a piccanin back to say that he was still 'talking about things' but would not be much longer. Eventually he returned and said that the matter had been well discussed by the men and they were agreeable to my taking photographs and would even co-operate with me, because they 'knew me', but that I had to 'soften them up first with something to drink'!

Knowing the Xhosa as I do, I was fortunately prepared for this and so the way was paved for my photographs.

The initiates had already been 'awakened' and were sitting in the cattle byre waiting with their blankets over their heads so that no married women could see them. Their piccanin *khankatha* at this stage has to do everything that the initiates do, so he was covered as well. When the time to start off came, they were made to stand up, but were told that they were not allowed to talk, because that would be disrespectful. They had to acknowledge their own 'littleness' since they were still not yet 'real' men.

The big *khankatha*, the *sosuthu* and another senior Xhosa man then marched the four covered figures back to their own hut which was about five hundred yards away. There, they had to drop their blankets and stand naked in front of the hut, while their blankets and all their eating utensils and even their pot were thrown inside the hut, where everything would be burned a little later on. I was most impressed with the beautiful build of the three young men and realised just how nature develops these people who live so close to her and whose work throughout their lives is physical. The *abakwetha* and their little lackey still did not speak a word and they acted like automatons on each instruction from those officiating.

Their first instruction was to turn and go to the river where they would wash themselves and get rid of their past. Some of the men present teased them and hit them with their sticks but they showed no emotion at all. They wore deadly serious expressions and nothing that was done to them had any effect whatsoever.

In some localities the initiates are chased to the river and beaten by the men present, but I specifically questioned Lolombela on this aspect and he said that, amongst his people, they were not. The march actually was a sedate and dignified affair with the three initiates and the little *khankatha* walking in single file to the river.

Once there, they were loudly lectured by the *sosuthu* and the *khankatha* and instructed to wash well so that they would remove their boyhood and would no longer be dogs, but

The Abakwetha "return home" in the
"coming out" ceremony after months in isolation.
Their faces are hidden so that they cannot see,
or be seen by, married women. The sticks they
carry have a special religious significance and
have been blackened by the smoke inside their hut.

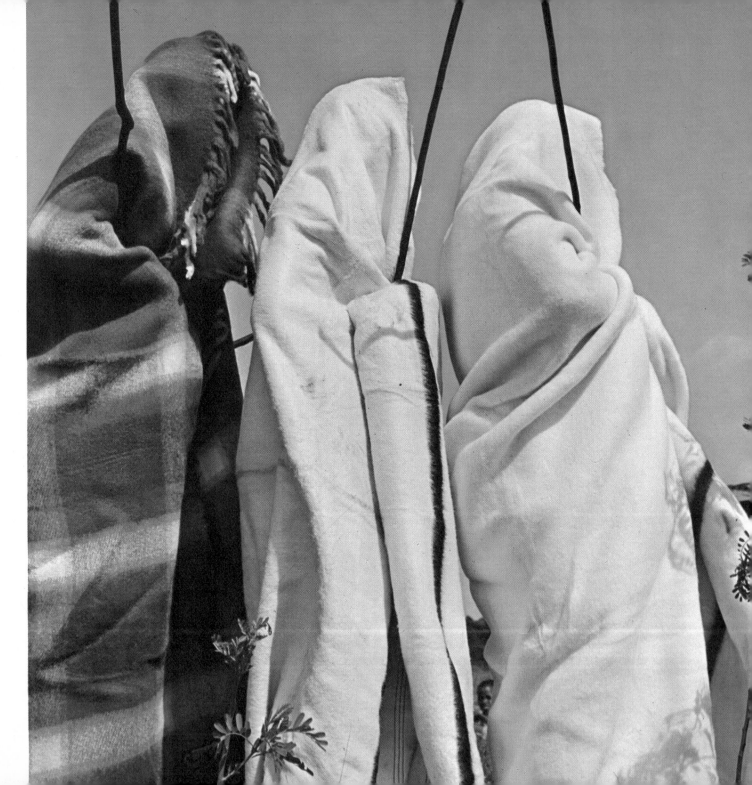

90

*After their anointing the Abakwetha prepare to go to the senior father's
home where the next phase of the initiation rite is performed. The blue
blanket has no significance except that it illustrates the encroachment of
Western civilisation.*

*Right: Their hut and all their possessions as Abakwetha burns.
The young men, as they go away in single file, may not, under any
circumstances, look back on the scene of their past.*

people and men. They were made to go straight into icy cold water and were given soap to clean all the white chalk from their bodies and they were even told just how to wash. At one stage, they were made to stand in a row in the water with the piccanin the last in the line and wash each other's backs. Each time they imagined they were clean enough and hoped to get out of the cold water they were made to go on but, at last, the *sosuthu* said 'That is all right! Now you are clean, we will go back and burn your hut.'

They did not dry themselves and were marched back in a row to the hut with the men prancing around them singing and attacking each other in mock battles. The initiates ignored everything that went on around them and did not speak at all or alter their expressions in any way.

The main part of the proceedings which followed at this stage was conducted by the *sosuthu*, a man always highly respected in the neighbourhood and a man in whose image the new men are supposed to mould their own lives. He must be honest and upright so that they will be like him and he must not be a wanderer or else *they* will wander.

Back at the little grass hut, the initiates and their lackey were lined up in a row and given four brand new blankets which were put at their feet, and from the straw on the inside of the hut, four knobkerries blackened by months of smoke were taken and put with the blankets. These sticks are of special significance and form part of their introduction to their new status in life.

The *sosuthu* at this point produced a pound of butter and said: 'I am going to anoint you with this fat', and thereupon took a handful and slapped it down roughly on top of the first initiate's head. He then brought it down over his face and down the centre of his chest to his legs from where he went down each leg separately to his feet. Thereafter he went back to the initiate's head and came down his back in the same way. Then he went on to the next in the line. The first initiate in the meantime proceeded to smear the butter over the rest of his body. The piccanin was smeared in the same way and all this happened without the initiates or the piccanin saying a single word. After this they were given sheaths of wild animal skin to put on with long tassels and were told to drape themselves in their new blankets and cover their heads. Then they were given their new sticks in the crook of their elbows and told to go away slowly, like 'small insignificant men should go', to the *sosuthu's* hut *without looking back* while their hut and their past burned behind them. By this time I had my cameras on tripods trained on the hut and one of the men very considerately came and told me that it was going to be very hot where I was (at least twenty-five yards from the hut) and that I should be careful of my cameras. I thought he was exaggerating until the men set fire to the dry thatch grass. Almost within seconds the hut was a roaring inferno. Fortunately my film was loaded and the camera ready, so all I had to do before hurrying further back was to click the shutter. I had thought it impossible that so much heat could be generated so quickly from a single small grass hut. It was tremendously dramatic and a most impressive sight.

When the flames had burned down low, the *sosuthu* brought out brandy and told the men to gather around. He looked at me enquiringly to see if I was going to add anything to their supply. Fortunately, again, I was prepared and they were delighted. Standing in a circle, they drank the liquor neat, smacked their lips and said, 'Now, let's go to the *sosuthu's* hut'.

When we arrived, the three initiates and the little *khankatha* were sitting in the hot sun on a grass mat in a row next to the cattle byre. Their blankets were wrapped around them and over their heads so they could not see or be seen by any married women. On one of the three, the thick blanket had opened a little over his forehead and I could see huge drops of perspiration standing out on him. The guests filed past and dropped small presents of money in the laps of the initiates, but the same person did not give to *each* initiate, only to the one in whom he had a personal interest. I heard one man tell one of the initiates that he was not giving him anything today but that he could come to his hut 'next week' and fetch a fowl. The old *sosuthu*, in his turn told his son that he could have 'that big brown goat'.

The *sosuthu* lectured the three and said that now they were *men*, and that they had to show respect to women and other men. They were no longer dogs and they had to lead a good life in future, with no more nonsense and no rascality and they must look after their parents as long as they lived and see that they never wanted for anything.

After this a spate of speeches started and everyone addressed everyone and the 'big' *khankatha* stood up and spoke at me in Xhosa, (very few Red Blankets speak English or Afrikaans).

'Men', he said, 'you all know Boss Aubrey. He has come a long way from the "place of gold" (to them Pretoria and Johannesburg is one place), to see this ceremony today. He knows it is an important event, just as we do, and he has taken photographs of it to put in a book so that everyone may know about it. He has "softened us up" nicely, he has treated us well and we hope that we, in turn, have helped him. We hope that all goes well with him. We greet you and thank you, Boss Aubrey.'

I knew I was expected to reply and that they would be disappointed in me if I did not.

'Men', I said, 'for a long time I have waited to see a ceremony like this and even if I had had to come from "the place of gold" twice, I still would have been here. Today, I have seen this thing you do and I see that it is good. I have heard how you have spoken to these young men, I have heard that the things you said were wise things. *Sosuthu*, I know now why they chose you to guide these young people. It is because there is goodness in your heart and you, *Khankatha*, I can see have done your job well, because these new men have played their part with dignity and respect. To you young men, I say, go now into this new world which you are entering, with strength in your hearts and with clean hands, and always remember to help other people in the way that is the custom of the Xhosa. I greet you all and wish you well.'

When the speeches were over, the initiates were told to rise and go with their faces hidden to a small hut so that the young girls of the kraal could smear them with red ochre.

In the hut, they were made to sit in a row and remove the covering from their faces, and then four girls came in with dishes of red ochre, mixed into a paste with water. The *khankatha* briskly ordered them to smear the faces, and then told the four to rise and drop their blankets. They did so and stood there naked. The girls briskly rubbed their bodies from head to foot with ochre over the thick grease which was still shining on them. The young men themselves helped and, when they were fully covered in ochre, the *khankatha* told them to turn their backs on the girls and rub the ochre from their bodies on to their new blankets. They did so, using the blankets as one would a bath towel and took off all the red ochre on to them. Then the whole process was started from the beginning again and repeated several more times until the blankets were completely red.

The turning of the bodies on the girls is to signify that they, the initiates, were now men and that, as such, would not be seen again naked in women's company.

After the blanket dyeing process the young men, who from now on would be known as *amakrwala**** (inexperienced, fresh, men), were painted 'nicely' and decorated around the eyes by the girls. They had beads put on them and a black cloth was closely wrapped around their heads. The *khankatha* then 'hid' the *amakrwala* in their red blankets and a can of beer was brought in and he gave each one a sip from the same can. After this they were made to pull their blankets up to their foreheads and their mothers and other married women were invited to file into the small hut to 'see' them for the first time. One of the mothers actually cried with emotion and the other two were obviously deeply impressed. Most of the women gave little presents and others promised pumpkins and maize and other things to eat if the *amakrwala* would come and fetch them later. To receive the presents, the girls gave each a white cotton 'smoking bag' which they hung up behind him. After the women had been past, the men followed suit and the newcomers who

---

* *Amakrwala* (plural), *Krwala* (singular). The 'r' in these words as in all Xhosa words, is pronounced as a 'g'.

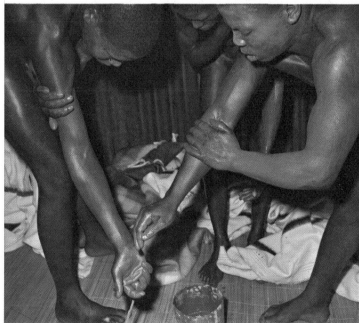
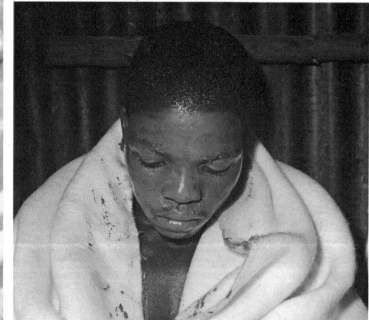

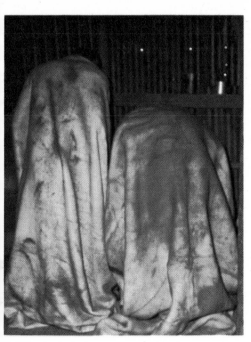

had not yet given presents made their donations.

After the last person had left the hut the *amakrwala* and the little *khankatha* were shut up in the dark and told they would not be allowed out unless it was necessary and then the big *khankatha* would come in and fetch them and he would take them out in a row, with the little *khankatha* at the end, to the cattle byre. The *khankatha* also reminded them that they were still only 'little men' and that they could not talk except, if necessary, in the softest whispers.

At this stage I decided there was no point in staying longer, and asked my guide, Lolombela, what the procedure would be from here on.

He said that the adults would continue drinking, eating and making merry until dark, when all the young un-married men and girls present, but not the *amakrwala*, would dance in their best beads. Then at the appointed time the latter would be brought out to parade to the cattle byre with their blankets tightly wrapped around their waists, and they would return to the hut again with their blankets up to their necks. They would be teased and pinched by the girls but they would not utter a sound. The next morning (Sunday) the *khankatha* would take them down to the river and make them wash well in the early light of dawn and when they got back to their hut the girls would be waiting to smear them red again and give them food and coffee. But, he said, 'the *amakrwala* at this stage do not like eating in front of anyone'. For the first time they would, then, be allowed to talk, but only softly, to the *khankatha* and to the girls, and they would discuss all the things that had happened to them. Then the girls would take out the *amakrwala's* short pipes with only four-inch stems* from their bags and the *amakrwala* would smoke for the first time.†

After this, Lolombela said, the new men with their blankets to their waists would be taken to all the other huts in the kraal and would have to dance for the crowd without talking. Then lastly, late on Sunday afternoon, the *khankatha*

would take each one of them back to his own home* and hand him over to his father saying: 'Here is your son, I give him back to you, he has not stolen and he has not done anything wrong.'

The father would then give the *khankatha* brandy as a present and thank him for keeping his son in good hands and the *khankatha* would reply: 'I have finished now' and he would go his own way. On the next morning, (Monday) the little *khankatha* would have to wash thoroughly at the river and resume *his* normal boyhood activities again.

The Life of the Krwala

The life of the new man for the following three months is one in which he continues to show respect and subservience. He has to talk softly and walk very slowly because, if he does not, he is 'boasting'. Every day at dawn he has to go down to the river to wash and, if he works for a farmer, he may leave the ochre off his body during the day but must smear his face, hands and feet. At night when he comes home he has to paint his whole body red again. He has to wear blue or green† earrings as part of his dress and beads on his head; if he is working, he may wear the white man's style of clothes but must always wear a hat.

Farmers are always hesitant to employ these newly-fledged men because they find the slow pace of their move-ments intolerable. Even if one is sent in a hurry to get stray cattle out of the mealie lands, he still cannot be induced to hurry and, only if he is behind a bush where no one can see him, is he allowed to speed up his movements.

At the end of three months all his 'krwala' clothes are given away and the young man gets others and then, after three years, he is expected to start looking around for a wife, but if he is a breadwinner in a family he may marry after two years, or, in exceptional cases, after one.

Far left: The Abakwetha *seated outside the "senior father's" hut where they listen to speeches intended to send them on their way into their new lives. Where previously, as boys, they were "dogs", they have now been united with their souls and have assumed the important role of manhood. Small presents are put on their laps with the blessings of well-wishers.*

Above left: Standing naked, the Abakwetha *are smeared all over with a paste of red ochre. Girls play a leading part in this procedure whereafter the* Abakwetha *emerge as "new" or "raw" men.*

Below left: In serious mood where he is not allowed to talk because he is "only a little man", an umkwetha *takes his part in the coming out ritual.*

Above: At periodic stages in which they and their new blankets are smeared red, the "raw men" turn their backs on the girls who smear them.*

---

* Xhosa women's pipes have stems about fifteen inches long.
† As boys, Xhosa do not officially smoke.

* All the proceedings took place at the *sosuthu's* (senior father's) hut.
† In the Xhosa language there is only one word for blue and green. If they have to specifically clarify which of the two it is, then they describe it either as the colour of the sky or of the grass. .

95

Chapter 7   The People of the River

A cavern on the seaward side of Cove Rock. Deep in this cavern, the mythical "People of the Sea or River" are said to live. "They have big spacious halls in there and their servant, the big amphibious monitor lizard, brings fresh cowdung from the land and smears the floor and walls for them."
On windy days when the sea comes crashing into the hollows of the cavern, the resulting thunder goes echoing up the coast . . . "that is them, talking on their drums".

There are many important and strong Xhosa beliefs of which even farmers and other white people who, in one way or another, have been associated with the tribe all their lives, have never heard. Or, if they have, then they know nothing more than that they exist. It is only when something dramatic related to a belief like this happens, and which the Xhosa concerned cannot keep to themselves, that the whole story comes to the surface.

The Xhosa belief in 'The People of the River' falls into this category, and I think there might have been nothing more than a passing reference to the 'People' in this book had not the event described at the end of this chapter brought 'them' forcibly to my notice and started a detailed research into the subject.

It is not that the Xhosa keep their ideas secret. They do not. But at the same time, they go about their own affairs quietly within their own circles and they keep Xhosa things to the Xhosa. They follow their own customs, make their sacrifices and hold séances with their witch-doctors as and when the occasion demands. These things are routine in their lives.

If a white man wants to know anything about the whys and wherefores of some current episode of a magical nature they will tell him—if he knows what questions to ask—except occasionally when they regard it as too awe-inspiring to talk about. Then they evade the questions for fear of upsetting the spirits or the influences concerned in the case.

Who The 'People' Are

To the Xhosa, the 'People of the River' exist as surely as does the family next door. They do not doubt that the 'People' are there down under the water where their homes are. The place where they sleep, even though it is under the water, is dry. Their home is a big place, they have in it their herds of goats and cattle, their dogs and fowls and, in fact, everything that the Xhosa themselves have on earth. When an earth person's animal is drowned and is never seen again, then it has been taken by the People of the River. But at the same time, the People's own animals also breed and multiply and at night they come out on to the grass lands above to eat.

The Xhosa say that the People of the River are the same size as humans and have long hair down to their shoulders, like the white people have, but their skin can be any colour . . . white, yellow or black. There are men, women and children and they have families and babies, but they do not wear clothes. Their wrists and ankles are 'soft' (a suggestion of flippers*), and because of this they cannot walk upright and so go around on all fours in the water. They cannot go any distance on the ground outside the water.

The People of the River are kind and good; they protect humans when they go swimming, which explains why a person rises in the water . . . he is being held up by 'them' so

---

* This description is that of a Gqunukwebe clansman living on the *coast* near to East London where his people are familiar with creatures of the sea. It is possible that other clans inland have different pictures in their minds.

that he will not drown. They become worried when earth people swim and so try to discourage them; that is why, on the beach, the waves come rushing up to anyone walking along the sand . . . 'the People are trying to chase him away from the dangers of the water'.

The Call of the 'People'

The Xhosa say that if the People of the River like someone, they sometimes 'call' him to come down to them. This is what happens when a person drowns and his body is not found – 'he has joined them'. In a death of this kind the Xhosa do not mourn because it is an honour to be chosen by *them*, and though the person is drowned 'he is not drowned'. The tribesmen believe that thereafter he is trained by the folk below as a witch-doctor of the most powerful kind and will be sent back to his kraal when the time is right to practice. Such a witch-doctor 'knows everything' and it is not possible ever to 'hide anything from him'.

If, on the other hand, someone drowns and his body is washed up, the explanation is that his death was an accident; the People did not call him at all, so they have sent him back. The tribe also takes account of the circumstances of a case when deciding whether the victim has been called or accidentally drowned. At the time I was investigating this subject, an aircraft crashed into the sea at Kayser's Beach (which is in territory where Xhosa live), with the loss of thirty-four lives. Though none of the bodies had been found at the time when I questioned Lolombela on the subject, he said: 'No, that was just an *accident*. Anyone can see that the "flying machine's" engine broke!'

Lolombela gave me a clear picture of the people of the river though, among his clan on the coast, they are known as the 'People of the Sea'. In fact Cove Rock, near where Lolombela lives, is said to be the home of the *chiefs* of the underwater people.

Cove Rock is an impressive place. A giant isolated rock, probably a hundred and fifty yards wide, set in a long stretch of golden sand, it is a landmark visible for many miles up and down the coast. Seven-eighths of its mass is in the sea and its peak rises to a height of perhaps a seven-storey building. And, at this point, it has split down from top to bottom and (seen from the shore) the left-hand portion has keeled over and settled low in the surf so that there is a wide gateway leading out to sea between the two parts. The major portion on the right has remained standing firm but the pounding seas and merciless winds have carved awesome tunnels and cavities into its side. Through the channel between the two parts the turbulent waters seethe back and forth restlessly and incessantly day and night, through high tide and low tide and through calm and storm. It is an awe-inspiring sight and it is easy to imagine why this rock has become a symbol in Xhosa mythology.

The Xhosa in those parts say that the channel between the two rocks is the gateway to the home of the underwater people. At night when the tide is high and the sea floods through it far up on to the beach, they believe that the People come with it to play in the shallow water on the sand. Once, many years ago, Lolombela says, one of them was left by the tide and could not get back to the water because 'they cannot walk far on dry land'. The next day a Xhosa man found him. The creature cried bitterly. He was full of sand and his usually-shiny skin was stiff and parched. In his language he begged and cried to be taken back to the water but the man could not understand him and, instead of doing so, carried him off to the farmer's home. The farmer in turn took him to the museum in East London and the Xhosa got R20 as a reward. 'But', Lolombela said, 'If only that Xhosa had used his brains and taken the creature back to the water, his fortune would have been made because the underwater people repay kindness with great and rich gifts.' He says they have different ways of returning kindness and, among others, they let the water wash a present up at a person's feet as he walks along the beach or beside the river. 'It looks just as if it happened by accident, but it is not an accident!'

In the sea, at the back of the main section of Cove Rock, the water has hewn large caverns into the stone and the sea comes pounding into them to send clouds of spray high up

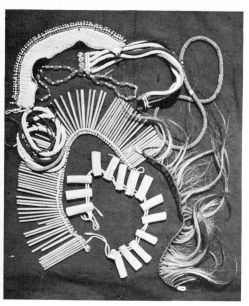

The neckwear of a young married woman is always conspicuous by its simplicity because she is still unimportant in status and she may not "boast". Nature provided the material for the main pieces here—the blocks are made from clay, the thinner lengths are stalks of dried river rushes and the piece at the side is from the tail brush of her "cow of the home".

into the air. The local Xhosa say these caverns are the doorways to the homes of the underwater folk. They say it is quite clear that the whole rock is hollow underneath because of the sound the water makes as it hits it. They think that the place below where 'they' sleep is quite dry, even though there is water all around.

Their picture of the People of the River or Sea, is clear and fixed in Xhosa minds; they are convinced that the 'others' even have the same customs—like the initiation to manhood ceremony or the *lobolo* marriage system—as the Xhosa themselves have. 'But, they eat the things of the sea like sand, fish and water' (they seem to have some idea of plankton), 'but sharks cannot harm them.'

As their domestic servant, the people of the water have the big amphibious monitor lizard which is about three or four feet in length. Their homes are smeared inside just like those of the Xhosa, but, as they themselves cannot go out on land to fetch cow dung for the purpose, they send the lizards. But the lizard has no hands like humans have to carry it, so he gathers it into a ball and rolls it down to the water's edge where the People take it from him.

The 'People's' Herds

Just as they have the same customs as the Xhosa, so they also have the same animals.

One man told me of his experience at Cove Rock one dark night when he saw some of their animals. He was so frightened, he said, that he will never again ever go back there in the dark.

He explained that his boss, who farms near the rock, and some of his friends went fishing there one night and he accompanied them to make coffee and to help them to carry their fishing tackle. He made coffee in the early part of the evening and took it to the fishermen at the water's edge. Then he came back and sat down alone near the fire. At first he kept it burning, but later it died down as he was a little lazy and the flames got lower and lower. He heard a twig snap near him (the rock has short scrub and bush growing on it) and he was certain that a black dog ran past on the scent of something. He took fright but reasoned the

dog must belong to one of the homesteads nearby. Then he heard the soft lowing of a cow and the sound of other animals and, against the skyline he saw the silhouette of cattle. Many of them. These were the herds of the People of the Sea coming out in the night to graze. They could not be anything else because no farmer's cattle could ever get down to the rock from the shore.

He was terrified and did not know where to run, so he piled big heaps of wood on the fire and sat as close as he could to it, waiting for the fishermen to come back. He felt hot, he sweated and he felt cold but kept on hearing sounds and seeing the cattle. That was the last time he went to the rock in the dark and he swears that he will never go there again.

Taboos

There are certain taboos and things a person must not do at *Gompo* (Cove Rock). Among other things, an expectant mother must never go near the place because it upsets the People. If for any reason she *has* to go there, then as she approaches, she must call out loudly to the People to ask their pardon and to explain why she has to go to the rock. Then they will excuse her but, if she does not do this, she will fall sick.

Another taboo is Xhosa magic medicine. It must never, under any circumstances, be taken near the People's home because they have their own much stronger medicines and, if someone brings his medicine to the place, there will be a clash of magic influences and the Xhosa will get hurt.

Their Pranks and Games

The People of the Sea or River are a happy folk and like enjoying themselves. On windy days when the sea comes crashing in at Cove Rock and its thunder goes echoing up the coast, the Xhosa insist that 'that is them talking on their drums'.

They are also said to have a keen sense of humour and one of their best-loved tricks is to tease humans. The Xhosa people at Cove Rock claim that, whenever anyone walks

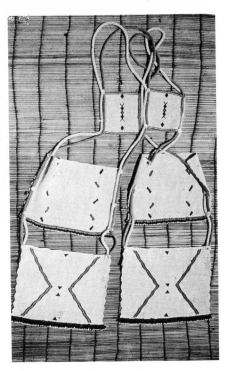

A particularly elaborate piece of beadwork.

past the rock, their hair stands on end and the skin tingles on their scalps because the 'People are staring at you'. (They illustrate how it is done by peering intently at something with an unflinching eye.)

'When the underwater people do this, it makes your hair stand and you shiver down your spine. Then the underwater people laugh till they fall over sideways. When they watch you, they hide behind rocks because they are *not* invisible like the sprite *Tikoloshe* is, but you must never, never, look one of them in the eye!'

Their idea of what will happen to anyone who is foolish enough to do so is a lovely example of Xhosa imagination at its best. Immediately, they say, his eyes and mouth will pull and distort to one side and stay like that, and he will only be able to see to one side and he will not be able to talk at all. The moment he arrives home, his family will at once know the reason for his state. Then the man's wife and his father must go straightaway to the place where the terrible thing happened and scream loudly at the water and towards the rock, taking care at the same time not to look into those eyes if they are still there. Then they must return home and talk to the afflicted person and he should then recover. If he does not, he must be taken to a witch-doctor or a specialist in magic medicines (herbalist) to be put right. Sometimes, in bad cases, it happens that neither of these treatments help and then the only thing left is to make an offering or sacrifice of a dark coloured ox to the People of the water.

The beast is killed and skinned at the water's edge and the whole carcase is left on the skin while the crowd retires and waits at a distance. The sea then comes in and takes the offering out with it . . . far, far out. Thereafter, half of the animal will be kept there to be eaten by the water people and the other half will be brought back by the waves to be eaten by the sick man and his family. Then his face will straighten and he will be completely cured.

Offerings to the 'People'

I have described the People of the River as physical beings who cannot make themselves invisible yet there appears to be another side to them which operates in the spiritual world. They can, for example, set up invisible protection around a homestead at night and bless its inhabitants with health and good fortune. It could be suggested that they do these things from a distance with their strong magic medicines (because Xhosa witches can work from a distance) but this does not coincide with the description of their activities around the home at night, which follows shortly. Instead, it seems, these are the work of the actual spirits of ancient ancestors who somehow manifest themselves in and through the People of the River.

If a Xhosa is questioned on a mysterious subject like this he invariably answers, 'I do not know, those are *their* ways but nobody knows *how* they do these things'.

I have mentioned that the People of the River are good and appreciative people, but I doubt whether many people outside of the Xhosa tribe realise that the Xhosa actually make offerings to them to gain their goodwill and to get the rewards of their gratitude. Alternatively, where a home is satisfied that they already have the blessings, they make an offering as a token of their appreciation for that protection.

Such sacrifices to the underwater folk differ fundamentally from almost all others made to the spirits of ancestors in that the meat on this occasion is not eaten soon after the animal is killed. The ritual of sacrifice is dealt with elsewhere in this book, but it does seem appropriate to discuss at this stage the specific form of the sacrifice made to the People of the River.

The animal, an ox or a goat, is killed in the afternoon inside the cattle kraal of the family making the offering, and it is skinned where it dies. The carcase is then left on its skin on the spot and when night falls, the family shut themselves in their huts and will not go outside again, not for anything until the next morning when it is light. As soon as it gets dark they say the People of the River come, apparently in spiritual form, and 'sit' around the carcase in a circle. They examine it minutely to satisfy themselves that it really is a good offering, and they take minute pieces of the meat which can hardly be noticed the next day. While 'they' are there nothing will come near that meat in the night, whether it is a jackal or a wild cat or dog. Nothing, and no one would be able to go near it, even if they tried, because a spell is over the offering. Even the people of the kraal themselves would not be able to approach it until day breaks and the spell lifts. All that night, the People of the River circle the home and the sacrifice and keep everything else away; then, if they are satisfied with the offering, they thereafter give their everlasting protection to the whole family and join the numbers of spiritual protectors of the homestead called *Izilo*.

Basically the *Izilo* are invisible wild animals into whom the spirits of ancestors come to look after the earthly family. (This subject is discussed in fuller detail elsewhere.)

A sacrifice made to the People of the River is repaid by them many times over. They are eternally grateful for such thoughtfulness and the Xhosa say that it is often quite unbelievable how they send gifts back to anyone who has made them an offering. For instance, they believe that a family might wake up in the morning and find a strange cow and calf in their kraal which they have never seen in their lives before. Without even questioning the miracle, they will know that it has been sent by *them*. The wonderful thing about such a cow is that she is always very fruitful and has many calves and her offspring too will flourish.

Another conspicuous occasion when the tribe makes an offering to the underwater people is when they set out to bring back to earth one of their number who has been drowned, and whose body has not been seen again. As has been described earlier, someone who is drowned in these circumstances has been 'called' by the 'People' who wish to train him as a witch-doctor. It is after such a period of training, and when an earthly witch-doctor tells the family that the man is now ready to come back, that an offering is made to bring him safely back to his own people.

This time the beast is killed at the water's edge and is, again, left on its skin, with a can of bantu beer left standing next to it so that the 'People' may drink. The Xhosa then retire to a distance and wait. The offering is then said to disappear into the water. After the People down below have taken from it all they need they put it back at the water's edge. The amazing thing about a carcase so returned, the Xhosa say, is the evidence in it of the strength of the magic of the People. They say that 'The meat does not even look as if it has been in the water and blood still oozes out of it!' Once the offering is back on land, the family collect it from the water's edge and take it to their home to eat. As they turn away from the water, they do not look back. Then, suddenly, while they are still on their way, and without knowing where he came from, they see in their midst the one who was drowned. He will look like he did before, but he will have been painted white, with chalk, by the People of the River and he will have magic powers beyond all understanding.

When he gets home, his people make him a special hut in which he lives quite alone but surrounded by a supply of his new and wonderful magic medicines.

Xhosa from all around flock to consult such a man and 'will pay anything' for his services because he knows everything after having been trained by the People of the River. There is no greater witch-doctor than such a man.

The Man who was 'Called'
The Xhosa belief in their magic and the mysteries that it encompasses holds tremendous power over their lives. Their ideas are sometimes so strong that once any particular mystical belief has dictated a course just about nothing, not even death, is allowed to interfere with it. Their inflexible faith in the People of the River actually claimed the life of a healthy married man at the time I was working on this book. The dramatic story of his self-inflicted end is set out below:

A young Xhosa man, but not the man in question, set out on foot one morning from King William's Town to go to a family near the Gonubie river, about twenty-five miles away. When he arrived in the late afternoon, great storm clouds were building up. Hot, tired and dusty, he decided to go down to a nearby dam to wash and freshen up. At that moment, the thunderstorm broke. As the young man put his hand on a metal gate at the side of the dam, he was struck dead by lightning.

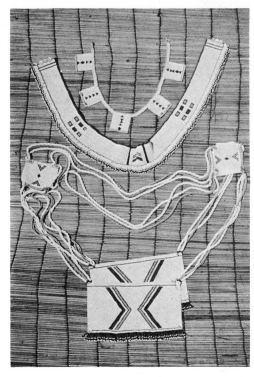

The pieces in this set including those on the opposite page and on the following two pages are all in the collection of one man. An interesting feature about the pieces is the consistency in the maker's theme and her affinity for geometrical designs.

Left : An individual piece from the collection shown on pages 100-103.

Right : Four belts worn all at once.

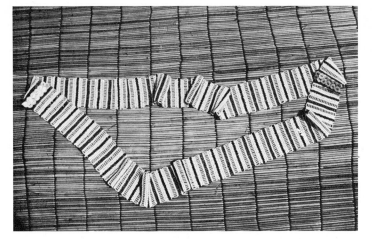

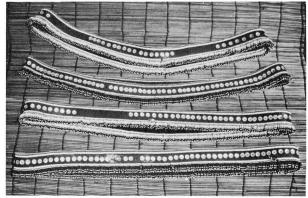

The event caused great consternation in the host's family. They were convinced that there was a significant message behind it and so decided to consult a witch-doctor.

First they called in a herbalist *(ixhwele)* to immunise each of them and the hut against any further trouble from lightning. The herbalist made the whole family strip naked in the dawn and wash themselves from head to foot with a cleansing medicine to rid them of the taint of the lightning. After that, each one had to rub an anti-lightning medicine over their bodies to keep away lightning in future. The hut, the cattle kraal and all the ground around the home were treated with medicines to stop the 'lightning bird', or *Impundulu,* from ever coming back again in future.

After this immunisation, the family and all their friends went off to see a witch-doctor to find out *why* the lightning had struck the young man. The witch-doctor communicated with the spirits that guide him, and was told that the death was a message from the People of the River, that the head of the host family had to go to them for training as a witch-doctor.

The host was satisfied that he had to answer the call but everyone knew he would come back at an appointed time.

On the day set aside, the man, his family and his friends went down to the Gonubie river. The spot chosen is a pool where the water is supposed to go down sheer from close to the bank. The place is said to be a home of the People of the River and it is where the man would meet them.

The crowd settled on the bank overlooking the water and the man stripped ready to enter the water. For some unexplained reason, he decided that his small daughter of about ten should accompany him, so she too dropped her clothes and held her father's hand as they entered the water. After only a few paces the child panicked and screamed and a man from the bank caught her and pulled her to safety. 'But', this man said, 'it was not easy, because something was pulling her from under the water.' Without emotion, her father went on and it was told by some of those present that, even though the water is very deep at that part, the man was only up to his waist until he reached the middle of the river and then, as if he had stepped from a precipice, he went straight down and out of sight. The water swirled over him and the ripples spread out across the river in ever-widening circles. His friends then threw in his clothes but they sank immediately into the depths where their owner had gone.

No one in the crowd wept, nor did the women wail as Xhosa women always do when someone dies. They all said it was now certain that the man really had been 'called' and that he would return as a great witch-doctor before long. Just *when* that time actually would be, no one knew but

102

Left: Anklets in which the beadwork is overlaid on goat skin.

Right: The piece on the middle left is a tie. It is unlikely that there is a message hidden in these simple designs since in those cases such symbols as doves (which could mean love) or cattle (which could relate, say, to riches or a marriage offering) are used.

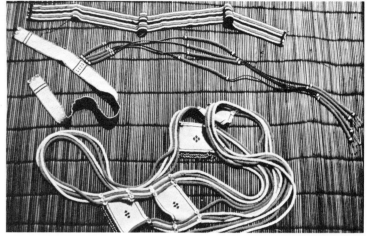

they did know that the local witch-doctor, who had guided them, would get a message in due course telling them to offer a dark-coloured ox at the water's edge to ensure a safe passage back for the new witch-doctor.

A white expert on Xhosa customs said that the drowned man had been shortsighted, because if he had swum underwater or made some plan to get out of the water unseen, so that he could re-appear at his kraal a few days later, he would have been famous and could have demanded any fees he liked as a witch-doctor. This Xhosa victim, however, had obviously been so sincere in his beliefs that he had not doubted his own safety or thought that his witch-doctor's guidance could be wrong.

The next day, the man's family had to explain his absence from work to their farmer employer. It is doubtful whether, except for this, the Xhosa would have told anyone outside their own people. The white man immediately reported the case to the police who searched for the body. This worried the Xhosa terribly 'because', they said, 'the workings of the People of the River should never be interfered with'. But no trace was found of the man even though skin-divers were brought to the scene from East London. The failure of the search relieved the Xhosa and they were more than satisfied that their friend was in the right hands.

There was no mourning, but every day someone went down to the river to see whether the man had not perhaps been thrown back by the people of the water as unsuitable material. Days went by, weeks and months and the family waited and their witch-doctor-adviser waited, but in the latter case, it was only for guidance telling him when to order the offering necessary to bring the man back. But this time was slow in coming. And then one day, after five months, the victim appeared floating face-downward on the surface of the pool. But, to ruin everything, the white farmer found him. Strangely enough, the body had not decomposed, due no doubt to the depth and coldness of the water.

The Xhosa said that if *only* the body had been found by one of *them*, everything would have been all right, they would have followed the proper rites, made an offering on the spot to the River People and the man would have returned to them alive as he was supposed to do.

As it happened, the white man called the police again and the body was dragged out. Dead. The man was buried on the banks of the river and his family went away sad and unhappy, while their friends shook their heads in pity that the works of the People of the River had been interfered with and the return process of the man to earth had been wrecked.

103

Chapter 8　　The Characters in Magic

A typical scene in the Xhosa districts of the Transkei where sledges dragged by oxen are used to transport the family's goods. Here, loads of thatch grass are brought home for a new hut.

Superstition among the Xhosa, as among all bantu tribes, is strong and is a part of their way of life. It is so important that they attribute most misfortune and illness, and anything for which they cannot find an explanation, to unnatural or supernatural influences. To combat such ills, they rely on magic, medicine and witchcraft. This is all part of the greater world in which they live, a world of witch-doctors, sprites, spirits and mysterious beings. Their life, furthermore, is full of taboos and they are strong believers in omens.

It would, however, perhaps be a little unfair to ridicule the uneducated Xhosa because of their superstitions or to judge them too harshly on this account, before giving some thought to the comparative superstitious beliefs of so many highly educated European people. There is the latter's fear of walking under a ladder; of thirteen at a table and of starting a journey on a Friday, just to mention a few.

The European's superstitions, like the Xhosa's, are based on the same illogical fear of the consequences, but those of the Xhosa are only more elaborate and more 'specialised'. In considering Xhosa beliefs which perhaps, in effect, can be regarded as negative or positive thoughts, one is led to wonder to what extent the power of the mind actually causes their thoughts to materialise into events.

If this does happen to any extent, then one begins to see how such happenings can consolidate a belief and make it into something strong enough to be accepted by uneducated and credulous minds as fact.

'People are Born Healthy'

The Xhosa say that people are born healthy. If anyone falls sick, it is because they have been bewitched or they have failed to make the proper sacrifices due to the spirits of their ancestors. Crop failures and other misfortunes, too, are often attributed to these causes. There are one or two exceptions to this belief. The Xhosa accept old age and accidents as a cause of death, and they also concede that certain foods can make people ill. To counter misfortune, they have built up elaborate magic procedures and developed all manner of medicines.

Magic

For purposes of this work I have attempted broadly to divide Xhosa magic, in so far as it concerns the casting of spells, into two categories, sorcery and witchcraft, or the work of sorcerers and the work of witches.* I purposely say 'broadly divide' because in actual fact there is not always a clear division between what is sorcery and what is witchcraft. Generally speaking, sorcery is the use of medicines of a *tangible* form to perpetrate the desired evil and witchcraft is the use of invisible agents, like water sprites and the lightning bird, for a similar purpose. These agents are known as familiars and they act on instructions from witches, either men or women, who 'send' them to do their mischief. Sorcerers and witches never do good, only evil.

* For purposes of this work a 'witch' may be either a man or a woman.

In the Xhosa world of magic and witchcraft, there are many characters like herbalists and sorcerers and witches, each with their own roles. The most important of these are described below but the witch-doctor, who is the person who 'smells-out' and finds witches, is discussed in a separate chapter.

The Herbalist—*Ixhwele*

The herbalist is an important person in Xhosa magic. He provides medicines for all purposes, to cure all sickness and ills and to immunise people and things against evil. He is regarded basically as a good person and uses his talents for the benefit of his clients, at his prices, but sometimes he is guilty of supplying medicine for nefarious purposes to sorcerers and others. His medicines are made from the most mysterious ingredients he can think up, and the more original his ideas are the more effective his medicines are likely to be. He uses such things as bats wings, crushed beetles, the fat of a puff-adder and genuine herbs. The nature of many of his ingredients is known only to himself. He even has medicine to immunise people and homes against lightning.

The Sorcerer— *Igqwira*

The Xhosa sorcerer is a man or woman who uses 'medicines' made from herbs and mysterious ingredients, to bring harm to property and people and even death to his enemies. The process of inflicting evil in this magic manner is known as *thakatha*, just as it is in witchcraft. The sorcerer may concoct his own medicines or sometimes obtain them from an unscrupulous herbalist.

Apart from herbs, he (or she) is said to use such things as the toes of a rat, ground and dried locusts and the burnt feathers of a black bird. Specific mixtures are concocted for specific purposes and the mixtures are used in different ways. If, for instance, it is wished to make an enemy's cattle sick, then a sorcerer will sprinkle his medicine in the gateway of the cattle kraal so that the animals will be bewitched as they walk over it, or as they inhale it. If, on the other hand, he

106

Left: The Cape Aloe (Aloe Ferox) *grows profusely in the Ciskei and is widely used by the Xhosa as a medicine for themselves and a remedy for "gall sickness" in their cattle.*

Below left: The "cortizone plant" or "elephant's foot" (Dioscorea Sylvatica): *another popular medicine, whose value the Xhosa probably learnt from the early Hottentots at the Cape.*

Below right: The leaves of this plant are used to bandage the wounds of the initiates to manhood (Abakwetha). *The author was unable to find out whether it has any healing properties or not.*

Right: This Euphorbia tree is said to grow on the site of an old Xhosa hut and that long ago another of its kind grew beside it. They were the sign of twins in the family.

wants to bring on a crop failure, he may make a fire next to the land and put medicines in it so that the wind takes the smoke across the fields and distributes the magic medicine over the crops so that they will not grow.

Sorcerers are believed to be able to 'send' things like lizards, scorpions or grasshoppers into people's stomachs and cause agonising discomfort and wind. But one of the most feared of all the sorcerers' instruments is the chameleon. The Xhosa are terrified of it because if *they* are 'sent into you', you get thinner and thinner and pine away and even die. They say that sorcerers grind up dry chameleons into a powder which they blow over a victim; he inhales it and 'it goes into his stomach'. After that has happened, the only person who can help the victim is a witch-doctor or a herbalist, who gives him medicine to drink (usually an emetic) to cleanse his system and rid him of the trouble. Some of the more clever witch-doctors are able to do even better than this because they can 'suck' the offending creature out through the skin of the sick one's stomach. To do this, the witch-doctor concocts some mixture which he places on the sore place; then he puts his two hands over that and sucks loudly between them until, with a triumphant exclamation, he produces some object, of any shape, which he has 'got out through the skin'. The frightened and super-stititous audience are always too afraid to look carefully at the 'thing', so they never know exactly what it looks like – but the important part is that they are convinced the trouble has been removed.

The Xhosa say that sorcerers can kill their enemies with medicines from a distance and without the person ever knowing what has happened to him. One man told me that when a sorcerer wants to do this, he mixes up medicines made specially for this purpose in a can and gets some of the person's hair or dirt from under his feet to put in the mixture. The sorcerer then spins a forked stick in the liquid and chants the man's name while he does so. The victim will then double up in agony, wherever he is, and fall down on the ground, unable to stand. He could die shortly after the ritual has been performed or even while it is still going on

Symbols of a well dressed man.

and he is unlikely to know that medicines have been used against him.

The extent to which the bantu allows his imagination to run riot in his belief in magic and the mysterious is well illustrated by the quotation given below from the book *Reaction to Conquest*, by Monica Hunter, which reads:–
'When a person is walking along a path he sees a snake. It rises up and bites him and soon he is dead. That snake is sent thus. The *Umthakathi** cuts a reed *(irwantsi)* and binds it with the sinews from the back of an *imamba* (the most deadly of South African snakes). He mixes rat droppings with the fat of an *isithunzela* (dead person raised by a wizard) and certain *amakhubalo* (charms). To give the snake teeth he adds needles. He calls the name of the person whom he wishes to kill, and puts the mixture on the road. It turns into an *imamba*, and will bite only the person whose name he has called. When the people look for the *imamba* after they have been bitten they see only sinews and needles–no snakes.'

Sorcery and the Love Potion

The Xhosa believe that love potions work and I have been told that they are used quite extensively by young men whose overtures have been rejected.

There are one or two variations in the manner in which they are supposed to be used, but two of the common ways are for the young man to put some magic medicine into food or in a soft sweet which he gives to the girl to eat, or else he stirs up a quantity in a can with a forked stick which he spins between the palms of his hands while he calls her name incessantly.

It is not always easy for a young man to get a supply of love potion because genuine herbalists are hesitant to give it to anyone. The danger is that the results can be so spectacular that the girl's father will know what has happened to her and makes the lover pay a heavy penalty in cattle and take the girl as his wife. That is, of course, assuming that the lover is a man eligible for marriage and to have a wife. If he

is an uncircumcised boy, his *father* would have to pay damages but the *boy*, no matter what his age, would still not be allowed by tribal law, to have the girl as his wife because uninitiated boys are not allowed to marry. I am told, however, that if a herbalist is satisfied that his customer is really in love with a girl, then he does give him some to use. The ingredients of a potion may differ but an important element is always something personal from the girl like sweat, dirt from under her feet or some of her hair.

When I made enquiries into the use of love potions from an old white man in the Macleantown district, where Xhosa traditions are still particularly strong, he insisted that he had actually experienced an incident in his early life of the effective use of a love potion. He said the young Xhosa man in question was very much in love with a girl who consistently rejected his approaches. The man was desperate and went to a herbalist for a supply of love potion. At first the herbalist refused, but his client was so sincere that in the end he agreed and gave it to him with details of how it should be used. This, it seems, consisted of sitting with a can of the mixture between his legs and spinning a forked stick in it while he called the girl's name over and over again. My informant said that all day the lover sat and spun and called while the unsuspecting girl worked in a farmer's house about two miles away. Then at last, as the sun was about to set, he saw her coming and, as she got closer, she started to run towards him. She came excitedly and then began to call his name and before she had even reached him she was professing her love. After this, she became hysterical and clung to him and screamed as she called his name. Everyone was very worried about her because she went on crying and seemed quite demented, clearly in a highly nervous state. My informant said her state continued for several days until the parents eventually got an antidote medicine for her from a herbalist. This calmed her but, he said, she was never the same again and always after that was somewhat unbalanced.

The Witch— *Igqwira*

The witch works with supernatural beings and spirits, and

---

* Person who 'sent' the snake–the witch.

Three women on their way home, with loads of firewood, stop for a rest and a smoke beside the cool water.

witchcraft extends the imagination even further than does sorcery. The agents used by witches are known as familiars. Some of them are most colourful beings and are quite spectacular in their performance. Perhaps the best known among them being the watersprite *Tikoloshe*, though the Lightning Bird *Impundulu*, does not lag far behind him.

Witches are said to 'keep' familiars and feed them and in return the familiar has to do the witch's evil bidding. The Xhosa are never very sure how a witch uses his or her familiar to bewitch but they say that at night, when everyone else is asleep, the witches 'send' them into people. In other cases, because the familiars can make themselves invisible, they are given medicines to put into people's food to make

them sick. This is an example of the intermingling of sorcery and witchcraft.

The Xhosa do not believe that witches gather together as an association at night or at any other time or that they work as an organisation. But they do say that they travel around together at night in a thing called a 'cage', which they can summon from the sky at will to take them to any faraway place they choose. In the early morning, before other people wake up, the 'cage' brings them back to their own homes and everyone thinks they have slept there all night. This 'vehicle' seems to be used more by women than by men, because men are believed to ride baboons (*imfene*) around on their errands. These baboons are kept hidden in

Stanley Cranes. In the days of their frontier wars against the white man (the 18th and 19th centuries) the Xhosa armies were known as the "Warriors of the Blue Crane Feathers" because their leaders and distinguished soldiers wore feathers from these "Blue" cranes in their hair. These two birds are in typical attitudes – the one in the foreground is in a resting position and the other is preening himself with one leg while standing on the other.

the bush or in a dark hut during the day, and at night are brought out to take the witches to wherever they wish to go. The Xhosa say that usually a man is a little heavy for his mount so, instead of sitting squarely on the baboon's back, he drags one of his own legs and helps the baboon along in that way. The baboon takes him over the roofs of houses and across the roughest country, and if anyone hears their dogs barking loudly and nervously at night, it is because a witch and his baboon are passing by.

The Xhosa imagination runs riot on their familiars and they conjure up all manner of weird ideas about them. Details of some of the best known familiars are given below. Often, ideas of just what a particular familiar is like differ from place to place, but the descriptions given here are those prevalent in the Ciskei.

Ichanti or *Umamlambo* (Mother of the River)

In some areas *Ichanti*, who is also referred to as *Inyoka* (snake), and *Umamlambo* are apparently thought to be different creatures, with the first-mentioned being the familiar of women and the second of men. But, in the Ciskei, they are one and the same thing. If he can be described as any one thing in particular, *Ichanti* is a water snake. In Xhosa magic, however, he can change himself into anything from an old kettle to an animal or a necklace and back to a snake at will. So *Ichanti* has no fixed shape. Because of this versatility, and his ability to disguise himself, the Xhosa are very much afraid of him, as they never know when he is around. When girls go down to the river to fetch water, they are always careful of anything strange that may be lying about, because if it is a 'snake' and it looks at them with its big round eyes or if it 'leans against them', they will go mad or even die.

On a farm near East London I had a first hand 'experience' of an *Ichanti* and the effect he has on the people who believe in him. At sunrise one morning, a young Xhosa man who was employed by the farmer came to the house where I was staying and told him how, in the middle of the night, he and his wife had heard a strange whistling sound coming up from the river. They knew it was an *ichanti*. It came nearer and

nearer, along the fence, towards their family hut where their children were asleep. The noise became louder, terrifying them but there was nothing they could do. They knew this *ichanti* had been 'sent' to bewitch them by someone who had a grudge against them. They heard it come in through the space under the old door, but they could not see it because it was dark and the fire was nearly dead. Then they heard it go to one of the children and blow into his nose and ears and they knew it had gone into his stomach. The man described how the child had awakened, screaming, its stomach churning with much wind. They knew that now its saliva and the liquids inside it would congeal into lumps. The man said the only way they could cure this child would be to get medicine from a herbalist and then for the whole family to leave the farm for ever. It was obvious that the person who had bewitched them wanted this, and that he or she would not let them rest now, unless they went away. In two days the family had left the farm.

Strangely enough, the Xhosa claim that the *ichanti* is one of the easier familiars to kill because *Thixo* (God) reveals him to you and then, if you have magic medicine made from the fat of another *ichanti* and its ground-up bones, you can make an *ichanti* powerless. They say that, in those circumstances, you will know when any suspicious thing is an *ichanti* and he will not be able to get away from you, so you can kill him with a stick or stab him with a knife. But if you have not got the medicine, then *Ichanti* will 'roll over and dodge' and you will not be able to kill him.

Impundulu

Impundulu is the lightning bird. He *is* the lightning. He is a spectacular fellow who stands upright and is about the size of a man. His feathers can be white or black and he has a hooked red beak and red legs with sharp talons, but these days he wears shoes to hide them. His weakness is women and despite his enormous power and strength, he can be something of a dandy where they are concerned. He can change himself into a man at will and has a smooth approach to the opposite sex. Sometimes, he may talk to a young girl

r a woman at the river when she goes to fetch water and
hen, with flattery and subtle compliments, he soon wins her
ffections and makes love to her. After this, he visits her
egularly, but from their associations, the Xhosa say,
hildren are never born because '*Impundulu* does not wish it'.
n this way, he becomes her familiar and she uses him to do
er witchcraft and sends him on her missions to make her
nemies sick.

The Xhosa people have different ideas on just *how*
mpundulu makes storms. One theory is that when he flaps
is wings he makes thunder and when he spits, that is the
ightning. They say that when he strikes, it is because he has
een sent by a witch to destroy an enemy or his property or
lse he is just amusing himself by 'kicking' someone. The
ower of the lightning bird is unlimited and I remember
hat, during the war years, an old Xhosa man told me one
ay that he could not understand why the white people were
ragging the war out so long when all they had to do was to
ngage a woman who 'kept' a lightning bird and then,
ogether, they could wipe out large crowds in no time.

The place where *Impundulu* strikes and tears up the ground
s where it lays its eggs and if you dig in that place you will
ind them. I heard an interesting little story in the Transkei
bout an *impundulu's* egg from an old trader who said that
ne day many years ago, when housewives used to put big
orcelain marbles into pots of boiling jam to stir it, a Xhosa
nan came furtively into the shop and looked around to see
f anyone was watching him. Then he sidled up to the trader
nd whispered that he wanted to show him something.
tealthily he fished one of the big marbles out from under
is red blanket and secretly showed it to him. This, he said,
vas an *impundulu's* egg which he had found in the veld. He
aid people would give him anything he asked for it, because
t was very strong magic which could be used to immunise
 hut against lightning. He would, he claimed, be able to
ell it to a witch-doctor or a herbalist for the price of a young
x at any time he liked.

Lolombela has told me that sometimes the lightning bird
hanges into a smartly dressed man in a black suit and red

tie (again a dandy) who mingles with a crowd and joins in conversations with the men. But sometimes he gives himself away in some small detail and makes his company suspicious of him. Then one of the men, pretending to act quite normally, goes off to fetch some beer for them to drink so that they can test *Impundulu,* who they know cannot drink it. When he is offered the drink and refuses with an excuse, the men rush at him with their sticks to kill him, but he is too clever for them and disappears into thin air. If, on the other hand, the men have been treated in advance with magic medicine against *Impundulu,* then he is powerless to move and stands in front of them quite paralysed and they are able to kill him. After that, they make special medicine from his fat and flesh which will immunise anyone against the strongest lightning; they can sell such medicine for a high price.

Tikoloshe or Hili

In Xhosa magic and in their folklore, probably the best-known character of all is *Tikoloshe,* the water sprite. He is also known as *Hili* (pronounced 'heelee').

In the minds of those who are not thoroughly conversant with the nature of this little character, *Tikoloshe* has a terrible reputation and is regarded as being really bad. But in reality, he is not. On the contrary, he is actually quite a lovable little character but he *is* terribly mischievous. He has a bad reputation because he is usually 'kept' by a woman who is a witch. He eats her boiled mealies and thick milk and he makes love to her, so that then he cannot say no when she sends him on her evil missions. It is in this way that his character and good name have both been ruined. He does wicked things very much against his own will. Sometimes, he cannot bring himself to make people sick or to destroy their cattle and then, in some clever way, he evades carrying out his mission.

Tikoloshe is a little fellow about two feet high. He is covered in grey hair and has a long grey beard down to his knees. He is not naturally invisible but he makes himself so with a little pebble which he keeps in his cheek or clenched in his hand. Because of his many enemies, he very seldom allows himself to be seen except by children, because they are his friends and he plays with them and protects them from danger. He always lives near rivers in eroded banks or in some such sheltered place and, like the People of the River and *Ichanti,* the monitor lizard is his servant. The lizard smears out his home for *Tikoloshe* and claps for him when he wants to dance.

Sometimes, when a witch wishes to kill off an enemy whom she has already made sick, she gives *Tikoloshe* medicine and tells him to take it along and put it in that person's food. If the victim is someone whom *Tikoloshe* likes because he allows him to suck milk from his cows and his dogs do not bark at him and *Tikoloshe* plays with his children, then the sprite will reveal himself to the person and tell him what he has been sent to do but, instead of giving him the poison, he gives him good medicine to make him better. But *Tikoloshe* knows that, next time, the witch will send *Impundulu* the lightning bird, so he also gives his friend an antidote with which to smear his hands and face against *Impundulu.* So, when *he* comes, the medicine will make *Impundulu* visible and paralysed in front of him. The man will then be able to get his assegai and stab the lightning bird to death. The would-be victim then cuts off a piece of his flesh and eats it, giving his wife and children each a piece to immunise them all against any further attacks. Their faces are also smeared with *Impundulu's* fat, and then the 'bird's' body is cut up and sold to witch-doctors and herbalists for a very good price. They, in their turn, use it to treat other people against lightning and the works of *Impundulu,* so that if ever he comes near them, he will immediately become visible and transfixed and easy to kill.

A witch who has failed with both *Tikoloshe* and the lightning bird might still try her luck with the river snake *Ichanti* (or *Inyoka*). But if she does, and the intended victim has been immunised and frightens *Ichanti* off before he can do any harm, then *Ichanti* in his rage might go back and kill her.

Another way in which a witch uses *Tikoloshe* for her

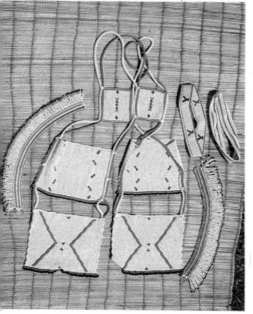

missions is to make him take *Ichanti* the snake on his shoulders to a hut at night. This is easy because both *Tikoloshe* and *Ichanti* make themselves invisible. Then *Tikoloshe* stands back while *Ichanti* kills the person and after that they both go back to their mistress.

It is said that *men* do not often use *Tikoloshe* as a familiar but, if they do, then their *Tikoloshe* is a female. Xhosa women, on the other hand, always keep a male *Tikoloshe*.

One man who told me about the activities of this little water sprite said :–

'Your wife might have a *Tikoloshe* and you would not know it because he can only be seen by her. When he sleeps with her at night and all is quiet and dark, and he thinks you are asleep, then *Tikoloshe* takes his stone of invisibility out of his mouth and puts it in his roll of plug tobacco under his wooden pillow. If you suspect your wife and you are clever, you will pretend to go to sleep at night, but you won't. Then, when you think *Tikoloshe* is asleep you open your eyes very, very slowly. When you see him, you jump up and grab your stick and stand against the door. Then you can do what you like with *Tikoloshe* and even kill him. Instead of killing him though, you might tell him you will spare his life, but from now on he has to work for *you*.'

Another man in the East London area told me a little story of how one hot day *Tikoloshe*, who loves swimming, put his stone of invisibility down on a rock and went into the river to swim. Up and down and back and forth he went happily, not knowing that a naughty piccanin was watching him from nearby. When *Tikoloshe* was at a safe distance, the piccanin quickly picked up the stone and himself became invisible. *Tikoloshe* was frantic. He rushed around grabbing in the direction of every snapping twig. But it was useless and the more he tried the more desperate he became. With his invisibility gone, he knew he was at the mercy of a vengeful world that had too many scores to settle with him. He was beside himself. Then the piccanin just stood still on a rock beside the water and kept quiet. *Tikoloshe* thought he had gone away, taking his stone with him. He broke down and cried bitterly so that great tears rolled down through

his beard and dripped to the ground. But his sobs were so sad that in the end the piccanin became sorry for him and gave the pebble back to *Tikoloshe*. 'Since then,' the man told me, '*Tikoloshe* is much more careful and takes fewer chances, and now he is seen even less than he ever was before.'

Tikoloshe's favourite diet is milk. He cannot resist it, and likes it so much that he often gets himself into trouble because of it. When the cows are shut up in the cattle kraal at night and their calves are in another pen nearby, *Tikoloshe* often goes along and milks a cow or two straight into his mouth to satisfy his craving for milk. But he knows that the next morning, when their owner comes out, he will notice that the cows have been milked so, to cover up, he lets all the calves out of their pen and leaves them with their mothers. Then the old Xhosa blames them. Sometimes, though, he overdoes this and the head of the homestead becomes suspicious and consults a herbalist *(ixhwele)* and asks him to trap the sprite with his magic medicines.

The Xhosa say that *Tikoloshe* always enters a cattle kraal from the back (and never through the gate) and that he also approaches a hut from the back, so the herbalist takes advantage of this and sets his trap in these areas. He sprinkles strong medicines in a circle where he knows the sprite is certain to walk, after which the herbalist's job is done, so he goes to bed and to sleep. If *Tikoloshe* walks into the trap in the night, he immediately becomes paralysed where he stands and he also becomes visible. He cannot move even a finger but if someone sees him and exclaims 'There is *Tikoloshe!*' then the spell breaks immediately and he vanishes back into invisibility and safety. So to avoid anyone upsetting his trap, the herbalist gets up very early the next morning before anyone else is about and himself disposes of the sprite, if he is there in the magic trap.

For this service the herbalist has to be paid several head of cattle but, what is even more important, he is allowed to keep *Tikoloshe's* body and from its fat and ground up bones he makes very potent 'medicine' which he sells at high prices. Among its many uses, such medicine is used to catch other *Tikoloshe* who are giving trouble.

Chapter 9   The Witch-Doctor

A young woman witch-doctor with the fur of a wild animal as her headdress. A witch-doctor's beads are always pure white, in keeping with their blanket-dress. This is a symbol of their purity.

In the chapter *The Characters in Magic*, I explained how the Xhosa see most sickness and nearly all ill-fortune as the work of sorcerers and witches. The present chapter is devoted to the other side of the scene, the witch-doctor *(Igqira)*. He is called in to find, or 'smell-out', a sorcerer or witch who is causing trouble and to give medicines to put matters right.

Difference Between a Herbalist and a Witch-doctor

It is perhaps worth noting here that there is a basic difference between the functions of the medicines of a herbalist *(Ixhwele)* and those of a witch-doctor *(Igqira)*. In theory, a herbalist is normally called in to *immunise* and *protect* with his medicines, whereas a witch-doctor *heals* with his. Herbalists, for instance, use medicine to 'doctor' kraals and people and their property, to protect them against the workings of *Tikoloshe* and *Impundulu* and other creatures working magic; witch-doctors heal people who have already been bewitched. I have specifically said that there is a difference 'in theory' between the functions of the medicines of herbalists and of witch-doctors because, in practice, there is frequently an overlap in the duties performed by these two characters, and witch-doctors may be found protecting mealie fields against crop failure and herbalists selling medicine to cure someone's cough.

There is no code of ethics to prevent either from trespassing in the other's field, so long as they have strong enough medicine for the work in hand.

Further, a herbalist's training, unlike that of a witch-doctor (i.e. diviner), which consists of spiritual tuition, is *physical*. He is taught the use of herbs and how to make other medicines by his father, in cases where he inherits the profession from him, or he can be taught by another herbalist over a number of years. Many herbalists have secret preparations of which only they know the contents, and to pass these on to their trainees they charge a fee which they think is proportionate to its value—and this can often be high.

Communion with Ancestral Spirits

The witch-doctor is a diviner who communes with ancestral spirits and gets guidance from them. He is also an intermediary between the living and the spirits of their deceased ancestors. In many cases, the Xhosa believe sickness is brought on by the displeasure of spirits to whom proper sacrifices have not been made, and here the witch-doctor gets a message from the spirits concerned explaining *why* they are displeased and what sacrifices they want to enable them to 'stay nicely' in place where they are.

The Training of a Witch-doctor

Witch-doctors are usually called to the profession by ancestral spirits. It sometimes happens that a father or more distant ancestor of a man or woman in life was a witch-doctor and then he calls the person concerned to the same profession. It can happen that a spirit who was not a witch-doctor on earth might still wish his descendant to take up the occupation.

Right: In the act of "smelling out" a witch who has been responsible for bringing sickness to the kraal. The audience here continues around to the left, in a circle, and the witch-doctor fires questions and suggestions at them in a game of "hot" or "cold". Timed handclapping follows each round.

Left: Watched by her assistant, whom she is training, the old witch-doctor spins a forked stick between her two palms to froth up the white "medicine". This procedure is followed for a variety of reasons—perhaps to clear evil spirits away from a séance or to make the witch-doctor's mind clear to "see things well".

The message from the spirit is as a rule manifested in the person concerned by a long illness, accompanied by peculiar behaviour, and consistent dreams of the imaginary wild animals which attach themselves to each Xhosa family, because spirits approach people on earth through them. When someone falls sick like this and dreams, his or her family consult a practising diviner (witch-doctor), who will assure them that these are definitely symptoms of the patient going into the initiate period of becoming a diviner (this state is known as *Ukuthwasa*). After this, the family and the person concerned have to decide whether or not he or she will train as a witch-doctor. This is a very serious stage in the person's life and involves a difficult decision, because witch-doctors are not always liked and sometimes have many enemies. Also, their lives are often very different from those of other tribesmen in that they have to spend

long periods out in the veld looking for herbs and medicines or they have to be away from their kraals on other business.

In these circumstances, people who are called, are often afraid to admit it and take it up – even though many Xhosa believe that anyone who disregards the call is liable to become ill and even die.

The procedure, once the decision to train as a diviner is made, is for the initiate or neophyte first to be healed by the diviner and then to be apprenticed to and live with him or her, and to learn the art of divining and of making and dispensing medicines. At an appropriate time in the training, a sacrifice is made to the spirits of the neophyte's ancestors which serves as food for them. This ensures that the new diviner is successful in his career. A neophyte's training is a long one and it may take several years before he is proclaimed capable of practising on his own account and even thereafter, he may, on occasion still find it necessary to go back to his tutor for guidance.

This training is the conventional one for a witch-doctor, but it will be recalled that in the chapter on the 'People of the River', I described how the greatest of all witch-doctors are those trained by the underwater people.

The most popular and best-known procedure or method by which the Xhosa witch-doctor divines is that known as 'Vumisa' but before discussing this in detail I propose to mention two other methods.

The 'Whistling' Witch-doctor

The first is the system of the 'Whistling witch-doctor'. He is supposedly a ventriloquist. This diviner claims that he has tiny little messengers called *Nomatotolo* – they are reputed to be about as big as olives – which he sends all around the world to find out what he wants to know. When he holds a séance, these messengers sit up in the thatch inside the hut where the witch-doctor works, while he asks them to find out whatever it is that is necessary. They speed away to do his bidding and are soon back again; and then the witch-doctor's audience can hear them talking to him in their little high-pitched 'whistling' voices. These diviners are not common but the Xhosa have an enormous amount of faith in them and, where they are available, the Xhosa will go to great lengths to acquire their services. The mystery of their powers apparently commands a great deal of respect and leaves the audience overawed.

The Thrower of Bones

The second type of diviner is the one who has a collection of bones, skulls, skins and other media with which he works. He has a special hut in which he keeps them and which he uses for his divining. I have been told of a diviner in the Komgha area, in Northern Ciskei near the Great Kei River, who works in this fashion. My informant, who had been present at one of his séances, says that the man arranged a collection of monkey, baboon and wild cat skulls and bones, small pieces of animal fur and many other strange items all around him on the floor of his hut. Then he jabbed an assegai into the ground in their midst, and while it stood there quivering, the diviner talked to the things and asked them all that he wanted to know. Apparently the direction in which the assegai shook indicated which of the bones or other items would answer him. As soon as the assegai stopped moving, the witch-doctor became silent and went into a trance while the bones 'answered him' and gave him the message of the ancestral spirits.

Vumisa

The third and common means of divining is the method known as *Vumisa*. In this, the witch-doctor sits in a circle formed by the men and women who have engaged him to smell out a witch, or perhaps to find stolen cattle, and he suggests to them why they have come. He is not told in advance why he has been asked to divine, as he has to find this out for himself and then give the audience the answer. For instance, he may start by saying: 'You have come about something with two legs,' and if he is *wrong* the audience clap and chant: 'We agree' ('*Siyavuma*'). Then he says: 'No! I am mistaken. It has got four legs.' If he is right the audience say: 'Throw behind' *(posa ngasemva)*, and their excitement warms up and the diviner gets his clue and goes on, 'It is a cow.' 'No it is an ox.' 'It is black,' or 'it is brown.' The excitement rises in the crowd.

'I can see, it is sick.'

The audience respond: 'Throw behind!'

And so he continues cleverly building up the image in his own mind of what the audience want him to tell them. Then he explains to them that 'the animal is sick because a witch in the neighbourhood sent *Tikoloshe* to "blow medicine over it"'. After this, he proceeds to smell out who the witch is and, here again, it is said he always accuses the person whom the audience themselves believe is guilty.

Witch-doctors do not always accuse the 'guilty' person outright but hint and, in an indirect manner, leave little doubt who it is. At other times, bolder diviners stand up and point a finger directly in the face of someone in the audience and say 'There is your witch!'

Such drama always stuns the crowd and they are shocked to find they really have a witch amongst them. The diviner does not say what penalty must be meted out to anyone found guilty, as that is a decision for the elders of a kraal, but he *is* likely to say that unless the witch is hounded out of the neighbourhood, the ills will never get better.

For this he charges one rand plus 2½ cents 'for tobacco!'

Appeal by the Accused

Anyone so 'smelled out' is always at liberty to appeal against the verdict and take his case to another witch-doctor for him to divine afresh, but opinions I have had from old Xhosa men on this re-opening of a case, are that, even though the accused is the witch-doctor's client, the decision can just as easily go against him a second time. The reason for this is perhaps that most witch-doctors consider it prudent to be guided by the popular will of the audience.

Tragedy of the Victim

The tragedy that can follow in the wake of a witch-doctor came to my notice in the lives of a young Xhosa couple I know from the Kei Road area. This incident illustrates the kind of fate that befalls someone accused of being a witch.

The young Xhosa husband, who is a particularly fine specimen of Xhosa manhood, took his wife in the traditional fashion, involving the payment of cattle *(lobolo)* to her father, and the two settled down as a normal newly-married man and wife. Then, in due course, she presented him with twins. The man had a brother living in the same area and, at the time the twins were born, two of the brother's children became ill with a complaint that lingered on so long that his family and others in the kraal became suspicious. They decided to engage a witch-doctor to find out the cause, because they were convinced that the children were bewitched.

In the séance that followed the diviner accused the young mother of the twins and said that she had bewitched the children because she was jealous of them.

The feelings of the men and women of the kraal rose to such a pitch that they outweighed any sense of reason and the woman had no chance. Her husband, like the rest, believed in the verdict and was convinced that there was nothing else for it but that she should go. He sent her and their children away to the home of another man in the family twenty miles away for him to look after.

In the circumstances of this case the young husband, according to Xhosa tradition, would have been quite within his rights if he had reclaimed at least part of his *lobolo* cattle back from her father, but he made no move in this direction because his only interest was to get clear at any cost of the evil that had come to his kraal.

The Witch-doctor's Habits

Xhosa witch-doctors always wear white. I have questioned many tribesmen on why this is so but, as in so many other cases involving traditions, they have long-since forgotten and simply say, 'they wear white because they are witch-doctors!' The actual reason, however, is said to be that white is the colour associated with ancestral spirits. It is a symbol of purity and of good. Black on the other hand is a sombre colour and one which signifies evil. It is a bad omen.

Right: The old witch-doctor and her retinue pause at the foot of historic Chief Ndlambe's throne before commencing a rain-making demonstration.

Left: An elder sits at the exact spot on the river bank where "the man who went down to meet the 'People of the River' sat before he walked into the water and disappeared".

As part of their dress, witch-doctors invariably wear a busby or high head-dress made from the fur of a wild animal and they carry some symbol of office like an antelope horn. Their beads are white.

Both sexes practice as witch-doctors in the tribe and probably just as many women follow the calling today as men.

When the Xhosa ask a witch-doctor to *vumisa* for them, they usually go to his hut. He seldom goes to theirs. The procedure is for the family who wish him to divine to get all the men and women of their kraal together and to go to his home. When they arrive, he does not come out immediately to meet them as that would be undignified, so the crowd sit down in a circle in front of his hut and wait. The atmosphere is tense because a séance is a serious thing and the minds of the crowd are always troubled with the idea that they have got a witch in their midst. In due course, the witch-doctor sends a messenger out to say that he will soon join them.

Then he comes rushing out of his hut and leaps into the midst of their circle, shouting and gesticulating and throwing his arms about wildly, until he is satisfied that he has created the necessary atmosphere and effect. Then he sits down in the circle where he has a good view of his audience and of their facial expressions and commences the proceedings.

Critics frequently comment on the dexterity with which a good diviner handles the circle and works his audience up to a feverish pitch and how, without their knowing, he draws from them the answers they *want* him to give. The crowd's excitement and spontaneous 'throw behind', when he hits the nail on the head, leaves him in no doubt of what he wants to know. Then, at the peak of the drama, he accuses the guilty one and leaves a pall of silence over the shocked crowd. Students of bantu custom often say that the group decide even before they leave home who is the witch among them, and that the diviner always accuses that person.

The Rainmaker

Certain witch-doctors specialise in particular callings and one that I met claimed that she could make rain. 'But,' she said, 'there is only one place in which the ceremony can be performed and that is at old Chief Ndlambe's stone at Macleantown.'

Ndlambe was a very well known chief who, in the beginning, was regent to his infant nephew Gaika, and later built up a following of his own, causing the white colonists a great deal of trouble in the Kaffir Wars. He died in the early 1800's and the clan of the Xhosa at Macleantown today still carry his name. Ndlambe's stone or throne as it is sometimes called, is a big rock overlooking deep valleys on two sides, and the Xhosa of the area say that the powerful Ndlambe used to sit on this rock with his followers below him and make his decrees and laws. The stone today is still well known to the Xhosa for many miles around.

The old witch-doctor said that, to make rain, it was necessary to sacrifice at the rock to the ancestral spirits a dark coloured ox, the colour of storm clouds—I omitted to ask her whether it was to Ndlambe's spirit in particular. This offering had to be accompanied by proper supplications and ritual dancing at the rock. She said that if I went along to the rock on a certain Sunday afternoon, she would show me how it was done. I accepted her offer, and at the appointed time she arrived dressed, in a white singlet with a flowing white skirt circled with rows of black braid around the bottom, a high busby of wild animal fur, a tobacco bag of the same fur and an 'apron' at her back made of tassels of animal skin. In her hand, as a symbol of her status, she carried a wild Gemsbuck horn at least three feet long. She was followed by a retinue consisting of an assistant witch-doctor whom she was training, her grown up son who is a pipemaker—he was adorned with masses of beads—and half a dozen women all very correctly dressed in their tribal clothes. Some inquisitive youths, wearing almost no clothes, brought up the rear. The latter had been indulging in their Sunday afternoon sport of fighting with knobkerries, and thought it might be more interesting to watch the witch-doctor than to get a sore head.

The old rainmaker lost no time. She led her following into a wild dance which was a remarkable demonstration of agility in one of her age and generous figure. To the accompaniment of hand-clapping and chanting, the rain-dancers leaped around in a succession of vigorous movements of hands, legs and bodies. The old witch-doctor completely dominated the scene with loud and noisy incantations to the clouds and to the sky and to the heavenly spirits until, sweating and panting, she slowly subsided and became quiet. Her retinue followed suit.

Then she looked at me and explained, 'Now if we had sacrificed an ox, in the proper way today, those white clouds you see there would by now be heavy and black and before you even got home, the rain would be coming down so that you could hardly see where you were going!'

Extra-Sensory Perception

Witch-hunting is the aspect of a witch-doctor's activities which receives most publicity, but he has another side which gives rise to speculation whether his kind do not at times really have extra-sensory perception and the power of 'seeing things'.

In the King William's Town area, when I was a boy, there lived a witch-doctor called Njajula who built up a reputation for divining that still lives today, some forty years after. He is still spoken of, not only among the Xhosa themselves but by old white farmers who knew him and had used his services to trace missing livestock. My father was a farmer and often spoke of his experiences with Njajula.

In those days of relatively poor communication in the outlying country districts and of less scientific farming and poor fences, the farmers often lost cattle, stolen or strayed, and stealing was easier then than it is now.

Under these conditions and knowing the ways of the Xhosa as they did, the farmers were in the habit of taking their Xhosa employees to a witch-doctor if they were suspicious that any stock they had lost had been stolen. The practice was a deterrent to thieving because all bantu are terrified of being 'smelled out' by a diviner.

Once my father lost, without trace, a litter of three well-bred spaniel puppies which were born on our farm. Their disappearance was a complete mystery and no one could throw any light on the incident, so my father decided to consult Njajula who lived some thirty miles away. In the séance which followed, Njajula, who had never been to the farm and had had no access to the audience (some of our farm staff) before it started, described in clear and accurate detail the homestead which he could 'see' and each building in the farmyard. Then he proceeded to animals . . . young animals . . . dogs . . . brown shiny dogs . . . 'but they were not alive, he could see them under some hay . . . they had wounds on their bodies, several wounds . . . deep wounds'. Then he said '. . . they have been stabbed dead with a pitchfork and hidden in a disused manger'.

Njajula went on to tell that 'the culprit is not in this audience. He is someone who left the farm several months ago in bad odour . . . he is not a good man . . . he came back in the night, when it was dark, to do this damage out of spite'.

My father got home and found the puppies where Njajula had told him they would be and all the details of the incident were found to be correct. Their killer was a man my father had discharged from his service some months before.

Others of the old farmers of his time who are still alive today, also tell how Njajula 'saw' animals which had strayed and fallen into ravines or mud holes and died. He did not go to the farms himself nor in many circumstances did he even know them but he often described the animals in detail, and where they would be found.

Njajula, it is said, passed on his calling to some of his sons and daughters but I have heard no reliable reports of how successfully they have kept up his tradition.

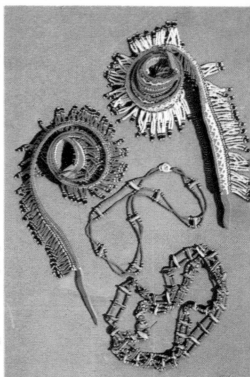

Chapter 10   Ancestor Worship

Far left: Dumane's collection of seventy-five individual pieces of beadwork. Each piece has a name.

Right: Various beadwork pieces in an unmarried girl's collection.

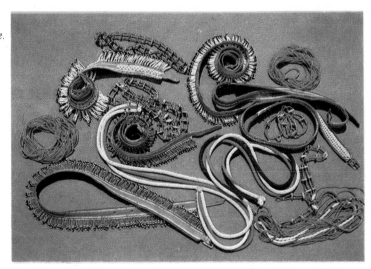

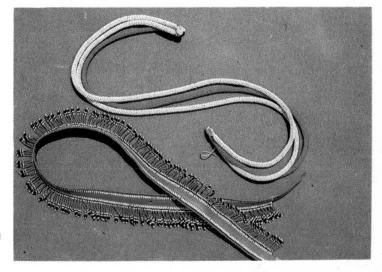

Ancestor Worship

Churches, shrines and images do not belong to the Red Blanket way of life. The Xhosa creed is ancestor worship and they pay homage to the spirits of their departed by the sacrifice of animals to them.

A Red Blanket is Never a Christian

A Xhosa wearing a red blanket is never a Christian because the moment he adopts christianity he abandons his tribal dress for the white man's clothes. A major reason for this is that much of the regalia of the tribesman is symbolic of magic in some form; it is therefore unchristian and so must be abandoned when christianity is accepted.

Once a Xhosa takes to the church he looks with scorn on his 'raw' brothers and strangely enough, the same applies in reverse. The Red Blanket is not intimidated. On the contrary, he remains proud to be a true tribesman and a follower of his peoples' traditions.

The religious beliefs of the red blanket Xhosa, even as they exist today, are well illustrated in the following extract from *Compendium of Kaffir Laws and Customs* by Colonel Maclean. It was written in 1855 and reads:–

'. . . they have very vague and indefinite ideas of a Supreme Being, and very confused notions of a future state; but that they recognise the immortality of the soul is evident from the fact that they believe in a supernatural agency, having an influence over the affairs of this life, such as health and sickness, prosperity and adversity, and to conciliate these overruling spirits they frequently sacrifice cattle to them. These spirits are supposed to be those of their ancestors.'

The Supreme Being—*Thixo*

The Supreme Being referred to is called *Thixo*. 'He made Heaven and earth and all the people and he is still there *somewhere*,' they do not know where . . . 'Perhaps he is in the clouds or even inside the earth,' they say. When a Xhosa has had a lucky escape from danger or death he exclaims: 'Ow! I was lucky, *Thixo* kept me' (meaning 'kept me safe'). But then, in the more general sense, where it concerns their everyday health or the prosperity of their cattle and crops, the Xhosa look more to the blessings of their ancestral spirits. Further, the spirits, being those of their own family, are closer to men and mean much more to the individual than does the all-powerful *Thixo* who watches over *all* his universe. The result in effect is that the cult of the Xhosa is that of ancestor worship. It is held by some that the sacrifices which are made by tribesmen are to *Thixo through* the spirits but in my opinion the average tribesman makes his offering to the departed heads of his family and thinks first and foremost, and probably exclusively, in their direction.

The Demands and Role of the Spirits

But even then, the part that the spirits themselves play is not really consistent with the idea that white people have of protective powers who love and guide and guard and keep. The Xhosa mind's first impression of their spirits appears to be that they, the spirits, want tributes and offerings made to them so that they can stay happily in the place where they are. All the subsequent behaviour of the spirits is tempered by these sacrifices, or absence of sacrifices, which are made to them. If sacrifices are not made or proper rites followed, the spirits become angry and bring sickness and other misfortunes, such as bad crops, on the family which has neglected

them. If, on the other hand, families on earth do pay proper homage then the spirits stay contented and multiply the family's herds and bring health and prosperity to their kraals. Spirits are only interested in their *own* families on earth and do not influence or in any way concern themselves with outsiders.

Even so, not all the spirits of the departed are capable of influencing the affairs of the living, because the spirits of young people and of those who had no authority on earth similarly have no power when they have moved into the spiritual world. The spirits who are the most important and have the most power, are those of the male head of a family and of his predecessors of the same standing. These spirits, furthermore, demand more important offerings from their families on earth at the time when they (the spirits) enter the spiritual world and then, thereafter, they frequently 'get hungry' for beer and meat. When this happens, it is essential that proper offerings are made to them because, if they are not placated, they vent their displeasure on the family.

Specific spirits have influence over specific people in a family and some are not able to be spirits to certain relatives whereas others are. An idea of the complexity of this aspect of the subject may be gathered from the following few lines from *Reaction to Conquest* by the well-known authority, Monica Hunter. This book is about the Pondo people but their basic beliefs about ancestors are similar to those of the Xhosa. Miss Hunter says: 'A man may be an *Ithongo** to his own or his brother's children, but not to a sister's children, and to his grand-children through his sons, but not to his daughters. A woman may be *Ithongo* to her own children, her sons' children, and to her brothers' children. Married women are under the influence of their own and their husbands' *amathongo†*. Neither man nor woman can influence their sisters' children who belong to different clans from themselves.'

It is interesting to note here that old people are regarded

---

* Spirit.
† Plural of *Ithongo*.

as spirits even before they die and sacrifices are actually made to them. In the same way, the living *head* of a family, even if he is still young, lends his spirit to work for the benefit of his family but, I have been told, his spirit may only work for their *good*–if he tries to bring about anything bad through his influence he will die.

The Family's Wild Animals

The manner in which spirits approach their people on earth is interesting. It is through the family's imaginary collection of 'wild animals' of which every family has a set. They look after that family and patrol around their huts at night and keep away any dangers which may approach. They are known as *Izilo*. I questioned Lolombela on the subject and he said that each family knows its own animals and that the same ones come down through the generations looking after their families. He told me that his family's animals were an elephant; a leopard; another animal which is 'like a leopard' but which I could not identify; a Cape bushbuck and another small antelope that is very rare. He said that his family had always had them. His statement interested me particularly in view of the fact that the elephant and the leopard at least have been extinct in even the near proximity to East London for a considerable time and I wondered whether his animals had in these circumstances been passed down in his family for perhaps upwards of a hundred years.

To approach people on earth, the ancestral spirits come to them through these wild animals and in this way make their will known. It seems that the Xhosa receive messages from the spirits by way of dreams which they have about the animals. The dreams are then interpreted by witch-doctors.

If someone is sick, for instance, the witch-doctor might tell the family that the spirits want that person to wear his or her necklace made from the tail brush of the cow of the home. If this is the decision, then no ceremony or prayer accompanies the act of putting the necklace on. This is because it is not necessary to tell the spirits anything. They know everything that goes on so no prayers are said. This principle is characteristic of all approaches to the spirits. It applies also to sacrifices made to spirits; here too the supplicants do not raise loud or wailing voices to heaven nor do they demonstrate in any spectacular way. They just talk to the spirits as if they were discussing something with a friend around the kraal fire, because the spirits know anyway what is the matter and what it is the people want of them.

A spirit might also transmit the message that he is not 'staying nicely' where he is because proper sacrifices have not been made to him and he is 'hungry for meat'. Then, after such a message, arrangements would be put in train to make the sacrifice. It often happens, however, that financial circumstances make it impossible to provide an ox or even the traditional white goat at short notice, in which case the family might save up for many years until they are able to procure a suitable animal. Once such a beast has been set aside, the family will not sell it at any price, no matter how much they need the money. The effect of so-earmarking it is that a pledge is made to the spirit concerned that the animal is *his* and will be killed for him at a suitable time. To dispose of it in any other way would be to court the intense displeasure of the spirit, with the resultant possibility of all manner of misfortune befalling his family on earth. I remember when I was a boy at home, my father often tried to buy such cattle when they were of good quality, as he felt he would be doing the family a favour by paying them a high price because they would then be able to sacrifice a less expensive animal and save some money, but his offers were never ever entertained. Since sacrifices are to the spirits of the departed from this world it seems appropriate, before discussing sacrificial rites in greater detail, to mention something of the Red Blanket Xhosa ideas on death.

Death and the Red Blanket

As mentioned elsewhere in this book, the Xhosa, with few exceptions, ascribe death to the work of witches and their magic. Probably as a result of this and death's link with magic, the Xhosa are afraid of the dead and regard their bodies as contaminating. As far as they can avoid it they will not touch a corpse. Immediately the breath leaves a person,

the women and girls of a kraal start wailing a loud and monotonous lament which at times almost reaches the pitch of hysteria. The burial takes place as soon as can be arranged but not later than the next day.

The only member of a family who has a specific place of burial is its head. He is buried under the brush at the back of the cattle byre from where he can watch over the cattle in the byre and also over the homestead. An alternative position is on the right hand side of the byre, but towards the back, as it is faced from the gateway. The brushes of the fence are removed for the grave to be dug and are put back in place on top of the grave on the day after the burial. The door of the hut and the gateway of the byre always face each other. Other members of a family are buried anywhere in the veld, 'it does not matter where'.

The tribal way of burial is for the corpse to be wrapped in a blanket and placed in a recessed shelf at the side in the bottom of a grave about four feet deep. Then stakes and stones are placed across the opening of the recess to stop the earth from filling it in. As the grave is filled, thorns are thrown in to prevent wild animals from digging and witches from tampering with the body for nefarious purposes.

Before anyone is buried, those officiating are always careful to ensure that nothing sharp or dangerous is buried with them because when they come back as spirits, and particularly if they are troublesome ones, they would be able to scratch or hurt those whom they 'visit'.
When anyone dies in a family, the other members shave their heads, but the only time clothes signifying mourning are worn is when the *head* of the family dies. Then his wife wears all black clothes for a month instead of her red ochre-dyed outfit. Similarly, on his death, the family hut is burnt to the ground, but for anyone else it is only freshly smeared out inside with cow dung.

It is perhaps of interest to note here that in the old days the Xhosa did not bury their dead. It was only in about the year 1818 that a prophet by the name of Makana, who built up a considerable reputation for his magical powers, decreed that from that time forth the dead should be buried. Those

who disobeyed this law, he said, would incur the wrath of the spirits. The custom caught on quickly and soon became general practice. Before this, those who were dying were taken to the bushes well away from the huts and deserted, while those who died in their huts were dragged away with rawhide thongs to some isolated place and discarded and their hut was burned.

Sacrifice to the Dead

The sacrifices offered after someone's death depend on the status they held in their family in their lifetime and on the ability of the family to afford the costs of offerings. While there are specific ritual sacrifices demanded of the deceased's own immediate family on earth, offerings are not limited to it only and it is common for members of the family in its other branches, who fall under the influence of the spirit of the particular departed, to make offerings to him. Such sacrifices may go on for many years after the person's death. The sacrifices mentioned below are, however, the obligatory ones made by the deceased's own family.

When I asked a man of the Gqunukwebe clan what sacrifices were made among his people, he said: 'For a child, we might kill a white goat but for the *head* of the family it is different . . . and it is very important. For him, within the first week we kill an ox. This,' he went on, 'is to make his spirit stay nicely in the new place to which it has gone. It is also to "wash the hands" and clean the contamination of death from those who touched the corpse when it was buried and from those who handled the person while he was still sick.

'Then, a second beast is killed after the widow has worn her mourning clothes for a month and has changed back to her red blankets. This one is to "turn the dead man in his grave".'

'The third offering,' he said 'must be of a beast from the dead man's own herd. It is made when the man has been dead a year. This is a very important sacrifice as it is to "sweep clean" the space between the front of the hut and the cattle byre and it is to make the spirit contented. It is also "to gather together the family's wild animals" *(Izilo)* and

Left: An elder of the Ndlambe clan here holds the horns of a steer he had sacrificed not long before to the spirit of his father "to make him stay nicely in the place to which he had gone".

Right: These tattoo marks are typical of those with which many Xhosa girls decorate their bodies. This girl's skin was cut with a razor blade by one of the men of her kraal and then pipe-oil was rubbed into the wounds to bring up the welts. She said "the oil burnt very much".

to make them satisfied because, if proper sacrifices are not made to them, they can be troublesome. They are the "animals" of our fathers and they must be kept contented if they are to look after the home well.'

In the chapter on the People of the River, I mentioned the offering made to the People and how the People themselves join the *Izilo* of the family and become the family's protectors. The third offering to the head of a family I have just described, takes the same form and partially serves the same purpose as does the offering to the People of the River. It brings the all-powerful 'animals' together. In this

offering, the same procedure of leaving the carcase in the kraal overnight is followed. During the night, all the *Izilo* come around and inspect it in the same way as the People of the River do in the sacrifice to them and nothing and no one will be able to come near the meat in the night.

Then, after sunrise the next morning, when the spell over the offering lifts, the host, who is the new head of the family, cuts a piece of meat from inside of the right front shoulder (they call this portion the *intsonyama*). He roasts this and gives a bit to each member of the deceased's immediate family to eat. After they have eaten, all the

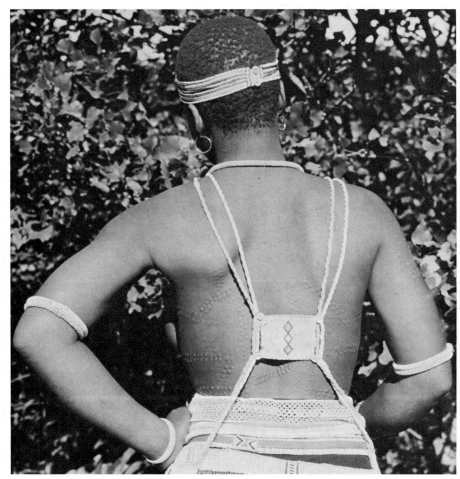

guests are allowed to join in the feast. All the meat at this particular sacrifice must be eaten at the homestead and none may be taken away. No one is specifically invited to attend but everyone around is expected to come and the feast goes on continuously for perhaps two days or more, until there is nothing left but bones. During the feasting the bones are kept in the animal's skin to prevent them from becoming defiled and after the feast is over they are burned to ashes.

The Choice of the Animal and Its Slaughter

The choice of an animal to be offered – except as mentioned above where a family saves up to buy one – is usually made by a witch-doctor after he has consulted with the spirits. Oxen or male goats are invariably chosen and I have not heard of an occasion where the female of either species is sacrificed. It may be an animal of which a member of the family has consistently dreamed, or the particular choice of the head of the family himself. As I mentioned earlier, once the animal has been set aside, no persuasion of any kind will induce the family to dispose of it in any other way.

In killing an animal, the basic procedures are the same, whether the offering is a supplication on behalf of a sick

Lolombela Mbangeli and his son Phopho Lolombela at Cove Rock. Many myths are attached by the Xhosa to this spectacular place and they say that at night the "People of the Sea" (or "River") come out on the sands here to play while "their" cattle graze on the scrub on its summit.

person or whether it is a ritual sacrifice for someone who has recently died. The finer details of procedure do, however, sometimes vary within clans or families because, they say, 'it is the custom of our people to do it this way.'

There are two principal ways of slaughtering an animal. The one is by a jab of a sharpened assegai in the back of the neck at the base of the skull, and the other is for the officiating priest (the head of the family) to insert his hand through a cut made in the living animal's belly below the ribs, and rip the aorta from the heart. Fortunately, with the advance of time, this latter method seems to have lost much of its appeal and is probably not practised very often now.

The first act in the sacrificial rite after the animal is dead is for the liver to be taken out. This is cut into two unequal portions and the bigger of the two is given to the men of the particular family making the offering, and the smaller to the women of the same family. Slits are cut on the one side of each piece and the two portions are roasted separately, with the slits on the underside, on the men and women's respective fires. While it roasts, the tripe of the dead animal is spread like a blanket over the liver and cooked with it. This early stage of the sacrificial rite is important because it embodies the actual act of giving sustenance to the spirit for whom the sacrifice has been made in that the fat and liquids, oozing out of the liver and hissing into the coals, represent the gift to him of 'the *meat* for which he has hungered'. This principle also applies to the juices from the rest of the meat when it is cooked.

I think it is appropriate to mention here that just as this 'meat' is offered, so the Xhosa offer other foods, beer and tobacco to their ancestors. For instance, when a man is drinking beer, he will spill a little on the ground at the far end of the cattle byre for his ancestors, before he takes a sip.

Similarly, before he picks up a coal out of the fire to light his pipe, he places some tobacco in the fire for the spirits to smoke. And so also with *any* other food; a Xhosa will be seen putting a fragment down on the ground, wherever he may be at the time, so that *they* may share with him. The Xhosa

---

* Xhosa women are never allowed to enter the byre. It is a place frequented by the spirits and is the sanctum of men.

say that the spirits do the same things as the living do.

Once the liver mentioned above is cooked, it is immediately eaten by the men and women of the sacrificing family and the tripe in turn is given to the children of the same family. The choicest parts of meat are always reserved for adults while the less choice parts are given to the children.

After the liver has been eaten, the next step is for meat to be taken from the inside of the right front shoulder for the sacrificing family to eat. This meat is known as the *intsonyama*. To obtain it, the carcase is laid on its backbone on its skin and held with the legs pointing upwards. It is then slit down between the shoulder and the ribs until the shoulder and leg fall sideways. A portion of flesh (the *intsonyama*) is then cut out from the inside of the shoulder and, after being roasted, is given, in small pieces, to each of the members of the family.

After this, the feasting is thrown open to all the guests and the revelry begins.

At the end of every sacrificial feast, it is customary to put the skull and horns of the animal in the fence of the cattle byre near the gate on the right hand side or to place them in the thatch inside the roof of the family hut above the door.

Whenever a sacrifice is made, the gall of the beast killed has an important role in that it is scattered over any blood that has been spilled on the ground in the course of the slaughtering. This is said to stop other cattle from coming later to bellow at the scene of the slaughter and from pawing at the grave (in the byre fence) of the late head of the family.

Before any animal dies, it must be made to bleat or bellow to call up the ancestral spirits. If it does not do so, it is not killed because this is a sign that it is not acceptable to the spirits as an offering. 'It is not what the spirits want.'

The Offering Which was Rejected

I once had the unusual experience of witnessing an offering which was not accepted by the spirits and I have often thought since that I was lucky not to have been caught up in the consequences.

It happened at the time when I first took up photography seriously but before I really knew much about a camera.

It was a Saturday afternoon and unfortunately for me – the amateur photographer – dull and overcast. I was at a farm about forty miles from East London when at the last minute I heard that one of the Xhosa families there was making an offering that afternoon to a family ancestor.

By the time I got to the kraal where the ceremony was to be held, armed with my camera and a pocket full of flash-bulbs, the offering, which was a young ox, was already lying trussed up on his side in the middle of the cattle byre. Standing over it with a sharp short-handled assegai in his right hand, was a powerfully built Xhosa man stripped to the waist. He stood firmly with bare legs splayed and the dusty manure pushing up between the toes of his hard, cracked feet. This was Dlamini, the present head of his family and the priest of the ceremony. The beast in front of him lay still but with eyes dilated and rolling white with fear.

Around Dlamini, stood four or five other men similarly stripped for work. They all wore turbans and some had modest mats of beads around their necks. The atmosphere was tense, the faces solemn. This was the presence of the spirits.

Outside the byre the flames of a new wood fire on which the *women** would ultimately roast their meat reached ten feet high or more. I knew that the men would later make their own fire *inside* the cattle byre on the right hand side towards the back of the byre, which is the spot dictated by the tribe's sacrificial rites. Beyond the fire sat a circle of women in their red-ochred outfits, beads and turbans. For once they were silent. To their left stood a group of teenage girls naked to the waist intently watching Dlamini's every move. Between them and the byre, and wearing even less, was a group of young boys who leaned on their knobkerries and waited, intently, expectantly.

This was the scene I, an outsider, came upon and not only came upon, but hoped to barge into with my blinding flashlights and noisy camera shutter. I did not know what move to make next. I was not sure that these people would even let me stay and watch, let alone take photographs. This ground was sacred to them and it was a solemn occasion.

They were 'with their ancestors,' so was it right for me to disturb them? Fortunately Dlamini knew me. He waited silently as I came quietly up to him. Opposite, an old man with a grey beard and equally grey hair watched with a stern expression on his old, lined face. I expected opposition from him and his word would have been important because elder men carry much respect among the Xhosa. I said quietly in Xhosa to Dlamini:
'I am very interested in this thing you are doing, will it be all right if I watch and take some photographs?'

He did not speak but looked enquiringly at his companions. The younger ones hesitated and looked in turn at the old one who then turned and spoke at me for the benefit of the others. In low, deliberate, authoritative tones, using his hands to emphasise his points, he said: 'When I was a young man, I worked for *his* father, who was Boss Charlie, at Ncera, where he farmed with sheep. Boss Aubrey, here, was a little boy then. That was two days on foot from here. Boss Aubrey does not know me, but I still remember him. He went away to school in town and then to the war and then he came back to the big town, Pretoria, near the goldfields (Johannesburg) and we have not seen him for many years. But today he is back in the country of the Xhosa. *I* know him and if he wants to take photos of the thing we do, then he must take them!'

He spat vehemently on the ground as if to emphasise his words and that he had had his say. Then he turned to me and added:
'But this is a big thing that we do here, you must not upset anything.'

I expressed my appreciation and moved back, for this was not the time for conversation.

Dlamini looked at his sharpened assegai and went forward. My camera flashlight went off and he stopped dead in his tracks. He had got a fright. The other men looked surprised, then annoyed. They had not expected *this* kind of photography and probably had never seen a flash-gun before but they quickly regained their dignity and ignored the incident. Dlamini bent down before the belly of the steer and the

*Xhosa women are never allowed to enter the byre. It is a place frequented by the spirits and is the sanctum of men.

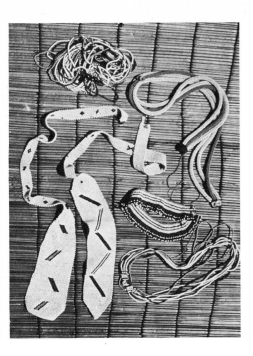

Ties made of beads and other sundry items in a man's collection.

others quickly switched their attention to him.

The sacrifice was about to be offered in proper ceremonial fashion.

Holding the assegai in the middle of its short shaft, and flatwise to the ground, he passed it back and forth in the air about a foot above the animal's body. Then he came down and passed it through between the trussed front legs then through between the back legs and a second time around the same way. The ox struggled to get up but the riems holding him only tightened and hurt and became more secure. He lay still again.

Before the animal could be killed it had to bellow to call the ancestral spirits and Dlamini now set out to get that call from the ox. From an inch away he suddenly jabbed the point of the assegai into its belly. The terrified animal emitted a snort and flung its head upwards. Its head stayed suspended for a moment and then crashed back with a sickening thud to the ground. Its trussed legs strained helplessly. Before it could recover Dlamini jabbed it again and a third time. It flung its head around wildly and missed a black leg by an inch as its owner leaped clear. It seemed as if the animal's bulging eyes would pop out of its head. Its nostrils blew up puffs of dusty manure and the man stuck it again and left another little white cut in its skin which quickly turned to red as another trickle of blood fell into the dust. But the terrified creature, with its eyes rolling wildly, did not bellow.

My flashgun broke the tension again and the men glanced quickly at the camera . . . was this the cause of the trouble? In that moment I was scared, but I knew I must not show it. I quickly took the hot bulb out of its holder and casually threw it to a piccanin standing nearby. He looked at it with unbelief . . . was this the thing that made such blinding sunlight? His friends crowded around him in excitement and the tension broke.

Dlamini wiped the red tip of his assegai between his left thumb and forefinger and blew the point, then he went around to the animal's head. I could not imagine what he was going to do then except perhaps kill it in desperation, but I should have known that superstition would never have allowed that before the spirits had been summoned.

Instead, Dlamini put the tip of the assegai up one of the animal's nostrils and spun it. Snorting with rage the animal blew out strings of blood-stained mucus. He struggled violently and if a knot had slipped anywhere in the riems, Dlamini might have paid with his life. But they held and the ox stubbornly did everything but bellow.

All this time I had been so pre-occupied, and horrified, watching the torture that I had not even thought to look at the faces around me. When I did, I think I saw the most serious and anxious faces I have ever seen. Except, that is, for the dozen piccanins who were still absorbed in the wonders of the bulb and were whispering among themselves.

Dlamini straightened up and quietly spoke to the man next to him who hurried out of the byre and into one of the huts. A moment later he came back with a can full of new, warm milk which he brought to Dlamini together with a forked stick about a foot long.

Dlamini was going to use magic to get rid of the evil influences which had upset the ceremony. He crouched on the ground and put the can between his legs and the shaft of the stick between the palms of his hands. He spun the fork vigorously in the milk until the froth rose in a thick foam up to the brim of the can. This to him looked like a good omen and Dlamini rose, took the assegai back from one of the men and returned to the trussed up ox.

He went through the torture all over again but the animal still stoically held out. It was having nothing to do with any spirits.

Obvious alarm spread through the crowds and low murmurs rose up all around and I saw, that day, what influence a strong head of a kraal has among his people. Dlamini turned slowly around and with a calm, unflinching stare, silenced every onlooker. Then he bent down and loosened the riems around the animal's legs. It kicked them loose and lay still for a moment as if unsure whether or not it was still bound, or perhaps its legs were too numb to move. Then it lifted its head and got shakily to its feet; swayed just once or twice and, with head down low walked slowly out of the gate . . . Free!

There was not a sound from the crowd. They knew that the spirits were displeased and their imaginations must have run riot in those moments of quietness.

I, myself, wondered as I watched the ox walk slowly out of sight behind the family hut what would happen now. I did not know whether the witch-doctor, when he had earmarked that particular ox, had nominated a second choice. But he had. I wondered too how many of these people thought that *I* might be responsible for upsetting the spirits, and I realised also that if anyone suggested at that moment that this was the case, there could be trouble. But slowly the tension subsided and the crowds started discussing the incident in hushed tones as they waited for the next move.

Dlamini called one of the young men who was standing nearby and curtly told him to fetch and bring in the other ox. This was a younger animal but equally fat and with strong, short horns. As he came in the gate he sensed trouble and broke into a trot. He ran nervously around the inside of the byre and, even though he obviously knew he could not clear the fence of mimosa brush, he tried a half-hearted jump but ended up caught in the dry thorny branches. The men caught him by the tail and pulled him out but the animal was not yet *ritually* caught and this now had to be done by lassoing his hind legs. To do this the men made two nooses from long riems and set them as snares flat in the middle of the byre with someone holding the end of each riem. Then the men harassed the animal in an attempt to get him to go into the trap. In its anxiety the ox raced in every direction but the right one, scattering men everywhere. The trap had to be reset time and time again before, at last the ox got a hind leg squarely in the noose which was whipped up to catch him. The second leg was easily caught.

The men then tied a noose of riem with a slip knot around the animal's belly and tugged. As the thong tightened, the ox caved in helplessly and came down on the ground, he was quite powerless, and was pushed over on to his side and trussed up.

Dlamini, with the assegai in his hand, confidently approached the offering and without wasting any time went into the same routine as he had used on the last occasion and the ox for its part, reacted in the same way as the other had. It was unbelievable. Dlamini tortured it in a frenzy and the ox snorted and sniffed and struggled as best it could but it stubbornly refused to bellow.

I could see this time that Dlamini could not control his fear. He looked nervously around as if in search of some comfort from his fellows but they were even more worried than he was. He turned again to the beast and half-heartedly and almost nervously, attacked it. One of the men asked if he should bring back the can of milk and the forked stick but, Dlamini shook his head and replied quietly: 'No! just loosen the ox and let it go!' He turned to another man and, giving him the assegai said: 'Here, take this to the hut and put it away'. He had not even cleaned the blood stains off of it.

The young steer got to its feet and ran out through the gate and as it did so lowered its head and kicked both back legs in the air almost as if in mock of its tormentors.

The crowds were hushed. They seemed too afraid to speak about the mystery and odd men and women in the crowd broke away and set off for home. The fire burned down low, the ashes heaped up and it was left unattended.

I waited quietly without making my presence felt and when the opportunity arose went to the old man who had earlier spoken up on my behalf.

'Madala' (old man), I said, 'What will happen now?'

He took his pipe out of his mouth, turned his old grey head to the side, and spat on the ground.

'Ow!' he said, 'This is an ugly thing. We can see that the spirits are not satisfied. They have not accepted our offerings, but we do not know why. As soon as we can, we will go to a witch-doctor and he will find out from the spirits what *they* want. Perhaps they wish to have a white goat *before* we sacrifice an ox, perhaps those were the wrong oxen . . . . We do not know, but when we find out, we will do the things they ask and they will be happy and contented in the place where they live and all will be well with us here on earth'.

Glossary of Xhosa Words

Abakwetha Plural of *Umkwetha*

Amakhubalo Charms

Amanzi Water

Doek (Iqhiya) A cloth used as a headdress, a turban

Hamba Go

Ibhasela A tip, a present

Ichanti A water snake with magic powers said by some to be same creature as *Umamlambo*

Igqira Witch-doctor, diviner

Igqwira Sorcerer, witch

Ikankatha The guardian at a boy's initiation to manhood school

Ikrwala 'A raw man' or male newly initiated to manhood

Ilobolo (Noun) The dowry or marriage payment to a bride's father

Imamba Type of snake – mamba

Imfene Baboon. Ridden by a witch (man) at night on nefarious missions

Impundulu The Lightning Bird

Intonjane Girl's initiation at or after puberty

Intsonyama The right shoulder (of the sacrificial animal)

Inyanga Moon

Inyoka Snake. In this case same as *Umamlambo*

Iqhiya Same as *Doek*

Isithunzela Dead person raised by a witch

Irwantsi Reed (a rush)

Ithongo Ancestral spirit

Ixhwele Herbalist

Izembe Axe

Izilo The spiritual 'wild animals' of a family

Nomatotolo Small imaginary flying objects which ventriloquist witch-doctors 'send' to distant parts to obtain information

'*Posa ngasemva*' 'Throw behind'. Terminology used at a witch-doctor's séance

'*Siyavuma*' 'We agree'. Terminology used at a witch-doctor's séance

Uhili Another name for *Tikoloshe* the water sprite

Ukuhlonipha To pay respect to someone e.g. by the use of substitute words

Ukulobola (Verb) to pay cattle for a girl taken in marriage

Ukumetsha To make love in a fashion prescribed by Xhosa tradition

Ukuthakatha To bewitch

Ukuthwala To carry off (a bride)

Ukutshila To dance the dance of the initiates to manhood

Ukuthwasa To be in the state of an initiate witch-doctor

Ukuxhentsa To dance the Xhosa dance

Ukuvumisa To divine – by a witch-doctor

Umkwetha (Singular) Initiate of manhood

Umamlambo 'Mother of the River' 'snake' used by witches, said to be same creature as *Ichanti*

Umthakathi One who bewitches (similar to *Igqwira*)

Umtshakazi A bride

Unongqause Anglicised version of *Unongqawuza*

Unongqawuza The tribe's national suicide of 1856, taken from the name of the prophetess who was initially responsible for it

Usosuthu 'Father of the kraal'. The senior father officiating at a boy's initiation to manhood ceremony

Uthekwane Hammerkop bird

Uthixo God. The Supreme Being

Utikoloshe The water sprite used as a familiar by witches

Ukwalusa Circumcision

Bibliography

BROWNLEE, The Hon. Charles, *Reminiscences of Kaffir Life and History*, Lovedale Mission Press, 1896.

HUNTER, Monica, *Reaction to Conquest*, Oxford University Press, 1936.

MACLEAN, Colonel C.B., (Compiled by Direction of), *A Compendium of Kaffir Laws and Customs*, Wesleyan Mission Press, Mount Coke, 1858.

SCHAPERA, I., (Edited by), *The Bantu-Speaking Tribes of South Africa*, Maskew Miller, 1937.

SOGA, J.H., *The Ama-Xhosa: Life and Customs*, Lovedale Press, 1932.

THEAL, George McCall, *History of South Africa*, Vols. 1-6, C. Struik, Cape Town.

Index of Main Subject Matter